Please God
Don't Let Me
Screw This Up!

Please God
Don't Let Me
Screw This Up!

Hope and Help from a Mom of Fifteen

Lyette Reback

fedd books

Fedd Books
P.O. Box 341973
Austin, TX 78734
www.thefeddagency.com
Published in association with The Fedd Agency, Inc., a
literary agency.
ISBN: 978-1-943217-01-4
eISBN: 978-1-943217-04-5

Library of Congress Control Number: 2015945169
Cover and Interior Design by Lauren Hall
Cover Photograph by Brian Schindler
Cover Photograph Edits by Jason Hedegard

Printed in the United States of America
First Edition 15 14 13 10 09 / 10 9 8 7 6 5 4 3 2 1

To David, the only man I could have walked this journey with.

CONTENTS

INTRODUCTION:
Please God Don't Let Me Screw This Up!

Twenty-one years old, I sat holding my six-day-old baby. I realized that, quite frankly, I had made a mess of my life up to now. The only thing I had gotten right so far was convincing this wonderful man next to me that I was a catch worth keeping, and somehow got him to marry me!

I was a handful as a kid—smart-mouthed and cute enough to talk my way out of most scrapes. I had walked through life about as gracefully as a bull in a china shop. Politely "released" from boarding school in 7th grade, I figured out real quick that what book smarts I lacked could be made up for with a bright smile and a vivacious personality. I returned to that same all-girls school as a sophomore and eventually graduated by the skin of my teeth, but not without wreaking complete havoc on all the staff of the boarding department and breaking enough of the "polite young lady rules" to cast me into a dungeon of despair. Outwardly, the light still shined brightly, but inwardly, the darkness was enveloping me.

The sins of my past came haunting as I stared into Daly Kay's perfectly innocent newborn face.

Oh, God.

Please *help*.

I can't allow her to feel these same pains I have brought upon myself. As I looked into her dark little eyes, the blackness of my own sins flooded my heart. Every mistake, every inflicted wound brought on by such foolish, youthful stupidity paraded itself in front of me as I beheld my precious daughter's beauty. All her purity seemed to only deepen my dirtiness.

Then I was reminded of all the times my mother had said, "I hope when you have a daughter, she is just like YOU!" Bless my mother's heart—she didn't mean that in a *good way*. She was hoping I would have some handful of a kid that would drive me just as nuts as I had driven her. At the time, I believed "bad parenting karma" was definitely out to get me. I was in big trouble.

So I shot forth a prayer to a God I *barely knew*

and *believed* He would hear me.

It wasn't fancy.

"Please God, don't let me screw this up!"

Hot tears were streaming down my face, covering Daly Kay's little cheeks. Call it postpartum baby blues, deliriousness, sleep deprivation, or the perfect cocktail of all three, but the reality was that I believed I needed to have been a good kid to get a good kid.

If that was true, I was doomed from the start. God knows, I wasn't a good kid. Not even close.

And now, here I was, just a young mom with a desperate desire to **do this job right**. God *did* hear me that day. Having Daly Kay is what brought me back to God, igniting a purpose that I didn't realize existed within me.

Having my first child taught me that the Creator of the Universe wants to hear from us! He isn't looking for perfection in us. He isn't even waiting around for us to be *good*. He just wants a relationship with us. If you have picked up this book, odds are you love your kids enough to know you don't have all the answers. Like me, you just don't want to screw this up. *This* being the lives of our children. *This* being the responsibility we have in preparing our children to face the world. It's a frightening prospect, I'll admit it. It scared the hell out of me for sure—quite literally.

I have seen it over and over again. God draws the hearts of many parents nearer to Him by the love they feel for their children.

He says to us, "See how much you love that child? Multiply that by infinity, and you get a small glimpse of how I feel about you!" Understanding this should give us boldness.

Twenty years and fifteen kids later, I am writing this book. I have now come to believe God wants to do amazing things through *all* of our children, in our *families*, and in our *nation*. I have learned He chooses "the foolish things of the world to put to shame the wise, and God has chosen the weak things of the world to put to shame the things which are mighty." (1 Corinthians 1:27 NKJV)

That's good news, folks! It means that if we're feeling stupid and weak when it comes to this whole parenting gig, we're probably exactly the kind of family He wants to use!

1.

Begin with the End in Mind

*I am God, and there is none like Me, Declaring the
end from the beginning...*
Isaiah 46:9-10 NKJV

When David and I were first married, we always
had a giant jigsaw puzzle in progress on our coffee table. For my highly active husband, the only
way I could get him to stop and really *talk* to me
was if I had some activity to distract him from the
fact that he was *actually* sitting still. We always
kept the box top photo right on the table. This
helped us know what colors went in what section.
Before we really began to work on the puzzle,
we separated out the pieces by colors that went
together in certain parts of the puzzle. We put all
the straight-edged pieces together. We placed the

corners at the edges and began to work our way from the outside in.

But the real key was that box top photo. Without it we would be clueless. The picture of what the finished product was supposed to look like was what made sense of the whole messy endeavor. David got some sort of deep-seated satisfaction from finishing a section of the puzzle as we talked through the events of the day.

The finished puzzle was more than just a bunch of pieces of cardboard on our coffee table. It represented the sum total of hours we had spent talking and dreaming about this new life we were beginning together.

Who isn't *puzzled* at the thought of raising another human being? Find me one adult who isn't the slightest bit ruffled at the daunting task of bringing a child up into adulthood. The sheer responsibility from *birth* to *self-sufficiency* is so broad—it's like a giant jigsaw puzzle. At the hospital, they hand you a newborn baby and it feels like they just scattered all five thousand pieces of the puzzle to the four corners of the earth. *How do we even start?*

Raising a child is a lot like putting that puzzle together. As we begin this grand task of raising an adult capable of succeeding at life and fulfilling their God-given purpose, **we must begin with the end in mind.**

It's often said that kids don't come with an instruction booklet. I've searched as hard as I can and found this to be true, unfortunately. After two decades of parenting and fifteen kids, I realized that maybe this was because the Good Lord wanted us to write our own.

I didn't know much as a new mom, but I knew a few things I wanted Daly Kay to have—and I knew the pitfalls I wanted her to avoid. Most of the hard knocks I had received growing up left scars I would rather my precious new baby never endure. With these few guidelines in mind I set out to define what minimums I wanted her to have before she flew our coop.

As parents, we all have hopes and dreams in mind for our children. It's never a bad thing to want the best for them. In fact, it reflects the very heart of a loving and gracious Heavenly Father! Because of this, the best place to start our own instruction manual is to begin with the end in mind by making a list of those hopes and dreams, both large and small, for our children. Begin to create that "box top picture" of who our children have the potential to become.

What do we want this child to have in terms

of faith, education, and capabilities? If we could draw a picture of this child in twenty years, what would he or she look like? (And please, if you are reading this book and have an older child, much of this still applies to you as a parent...don't lose hope. *Hear me out.*) Whether we have a newborn or if we are just beginning this journey in terms of refocusing our parenting efforts into something more productive and fruitful, at first we must approach with the end in our sights—with the basic guidelines we hope to achieve in mind. Print inspiring photos of people in the line of work your child desires to pursue and place the child's photo alongside. This is a small and effective way to provide inspiration for our kids.

For the most part, many of us would start our list out with some very similar attributes:

- A faith-filled individual
- A healthy young adult
- An education
- Competitive in the best sense of the word
- Talents and skills developed
- A child who perseveres, works diligently

The list from there probably varies and widens as we consider our own family histories, experiences, and, of course, as the child develops and begins to display all kinds of possibilities. Let me just give some examples of the basics to show you how to begin with the end in mind.

I want a healthy child.
I will feed my children nutritious foods. I'll make it a point to spend time outdoors. I'll become a good example in terms of physical fitness and include them just by jogging with them in the stroller or as they ride their bike alongside me. Map out what *healthy* looks like for your family. Make goals and guidelines, and make plans to work toward those goals. It can be as simple as including the children in your own pursuit of physical fitness. Who knows—one day, by your example, you may discover that you have a talented, God-gifted athlete growing right under your roof! See how easy it is to start small?

I was never much of a hard-core athlete as a kiddo, but I married into a crazy triathlon family. I began running when I met my husband and as the babies came I would spend the first part of our day right after breakfast pushing them around in a jogger while I ran. The road behind us was littered with peanuts the children would throw to the squirrels and cheerios they would snack on

5

as we ran our daily route. Eventually I ran a few marathons and for the last five years, my girls over the age of fourteen have been running the Disney Princess Half Marathon with me! I started small by pushing them in a jogger so I could get back into shape, but it made them love the sport and now they compete, too.

I want a child with a good education.
I'll start by reading to them every day. I'll think ahead about what "getting a good education" will require of me, of the child, and begin lining up whatever it takes to accomplish that. I begin to educate myself on the different schools and options available. For our family, homeschooling became the best option. Education is a broad spectrum with so many possibilities. Become familiar with what education will look like for your family. Begin to think about how you can save for college. A wise parent looks ahead and considers carefully what opportunities they can begin to work toward for their child.

When Daly Kay was just a few days old, in my postpartum delirium I was inconsolable and terrified. I remember thinking the only good gift I could give this little baby was a good education. David, in an effort to calm his wife and stem my river of tears, ran helplessly to the bank and invested in the Florida Prepaid college tuition program. He came home and held out the brochure as a sacrificial peace offering. It helped. I rested easier knowing my girl could go to school come what may. Sometimes a new mama doesn't make much sense, but wise is the man who does what he can to comfort her. Eventually Daly Kay went on to graduate high school and get her bachelors degree in Liberal Arts simultaneously by the age of eighteen.

I want a child filled with faith.

I must evaluate honestly where I stand. If I want my kids to know God, then I need to get acquainted with Him as well! It's imperative that I find a church, and get into a friendship with someone a little bit further down the road on their faith journey. Sometimes we have fallen so far away from our relationship with God that we are hesitant to go back...which our loving Heavenly Father never wants us to believe! Perhaps we fear our kids will ask us questions we can't answer...which of course they will and we just have to go about finding the answers together. Having a child who walks in faith as an adult is the goal, but along the way, we find it is our children who drive us deeper into our faith than anything else ever could. Walk and learn together. It's a beautiful journey. As I said before, having Daly Kay is what really began my walk of faith.

Even If You Can't See Clearly, You Can Still Have a Clear Vision

Several months ago, we took the children to hear Gail McWilliams speak. Gail shared that, years ago during her second pregnancy, the doctor told her she would have to choose between continuing with her pregnancy or keeping her eyesight. With certain blindness ahead, she chose to keep her baby. One of the most powerful statements she shared with the audience was, "I've learned even if you can't see clearly, you can still have a clear vision." Gail knew she could have a clear vision for what she wanted her future and those of her children to look like. How applicable to all of us parents!

Often, we are "in the weeds." We are so busy with the crazy life of tiny tots, tweens, or teens that we can barely see right in front of us. Maybe we miss some fairly simple things we need to work on with our kiddos because they are always right under our noses. It's during these times that a helpful word from a coach or teacher can encourage us to focus on an aspect of our child's character training that we may have previously overlooked. But even in the busiest stages of life, we can still have a clear vision for our child's future. We can still know where we want to end up as a family even if at this particular point in time we haven't even begun to map out how to get there.

Are You a Reactionary or a Visionary Parent?

Parenting can be summed up into two basic modes of thinking. There are reactionaries and visionaries.

Reactionaries are the parents who just survive going day to day. No plan, no specific goals...just making it from one month of the calendar to the next. These parents are generally overwhelmed, exhausted, outgunned, undermanned, and strategically outmaneuvered on a consistent basis by a basic three-year-old. Why? Because a three-year-old knows what she wants and will be completely shameless in going about getting it. Reactionary parents "lose it" frequently and their discipline can border on abusive because the punishment is a reaction born out of out of anger aimed at a child who has no clear boundaries and no known consistent consequences. The child, be they six or sixteen, never knows what (if any) punishment may ensue because the reactionary parent has no plan or strategy. Being late for curfew could garner a grounding this week, be ignored the next week, and get a firm slap in the face the week following that. Reactionary is obviously not the ideal way to go.

Visionary parents, on the other hand, seldom have knee-jerk reactions because they have a long-term plan. Their goals for junior are well laid. They make a plan and begin to implement it in terms of character training, education, and discipline. The plans may change from time to time, but the vision and the mission never does.

The visionary parent will not always be perfect in disciplining their child, but they have clearly defined "dos and don'ts." If junior crosses those lines, then junior chose the repercussions that were well known to him ahead of breaking those guidelines...not mom and dad disciplining on a whim and in anger like the reactionary parent.

Visionary parents are relentless in their pursuit of what is best for and in their child. Like the shameless three-year-old bent on getting his way, a visionary parent never gives up the fight because they look down the road frequently enough to see just how high the stakes are.

Visionary parents have stronger marriages because they are working on these goals together as husband and wife, as mom and dad, and as a family.

Visionary parents will look at idiosyncrasies within a child's scope of behavior and ask God for wisdom on why He put those into their son or daughter. How do these challenges help this child in becoming who God created him to be? Wisely, they will train up this child in the way he should go. They will not seek to simply have a well-behaved, obedient citizen, but they desire to raise an equipped soldier in God's army.

It's important as parents that we evaluate ourselves. In our parenting, are we reactionary or visionary? Do we have knee-jerk reactions to our child's misbehaviors that are less than pretty? Or are we a visionary—dealing head-on with today's challenges and planning, while believing God's best for our child and his future?

Two Major Factors of Visionary Parenting

The key to being a visionary parent boils down to

two things...both symbiotic.

Priorities and routine.

Anyone who has had a baby knows the feeling....

"When did I last feed the baby?"

"Did I change the baby after that feeding?"

"What time is it?" Or better yet, "What **DAY** is it?"

"Did the baby just sleep four hours or did I get up and feed him? I can't remember!"

Folks, our best bet for making it through any stage of parenting, our most helpful and basic tool, is a routine. Without a routine, we are not guaranteed a meal, a shower, or even time to run to the bathroom! Our lives with one newborn or three teenagers can feel completely out of control, and we can be smothered by the tyranny of the urgent. Without priorities and a routine we will be at the whim of everyone's emergencies and we will spend our days putting out fires and our nights will be sleepless.

I am by no means a clock-watcher. I would never decide against feeding a child until a certain time, but I do keep a pretty steady flow to the days around my home so that everyone, especially me, knows what to expect. This breeds comfort and security. By prioritizing needs and sticking to a routine, we can have a written idea of how our day will go. Inside our plan we include the vital things for our children and ourselves. If we have wee ones, we ensure that we have time to read, play, nap, go outside, and snuggle before bed. With our tweens we prioritize family time, school, and athletics. We also make time for the things we as parents need to do—a quiet time, showering (and in my case, plenty of MAKE UP), getting dressed, exercise, cooking, cleaning, and reading. Without a plan, we soon find we spend an inordinate amount of time on baby and get nothing accomplished for ourselves, hubby, work, or home. Or we spend all of our time on ourselves, and our other areas of work and ministry are not at all cared for. Many of our roles as wife, mother, daughter, friend, or co-worker can become neglected.

Plan. Prioritize. Strategize. Make the most of each day by using a consistent routine to accomplish everything needed. Without a routine, our days become a series of emergencies instead of a purpose-filled accomplishment. Simple things like reading to little ones, playing board games, and even enjoying a new recipe, fall by the wayside because we did not plan to make time for these things.

If we begin with the end in mind, focus on being

a visionary parent, prioritize, lay out routines, plans, and goals, and keep that finished picture of the puzzle in front of us, we will succeed. My one prayer twenty years ago with little newborn Daly Kay in my hands, and the countless prayers and mistakes I have made since, have taught me these basic truths.

Drawing a Line in the Sand

I remember the moment as clear as if it were yesterday. David and I had decided to homeschool. At the time I had four little girls and my oldest, Daly Kay, was six. I was organizing the playroom into a schoolroom, hanging up a bulletin board. I recall the precarious way I was leaning over a bookshelf in an attempt to nail in the picture-hanging hook. I can still see the room exactly as it stood at that moment, wearing my classic pink and green Lilly Pulitzer shift dress. Running through my mind were all the thoughts and dreams I held for my oldest daughter. As I placed the finishing touches on our classroom, I was considering the kind of woman I hoped Daly Kay would become.

"**YOU must become that kind of woman first,**" a voice inside my head spoke so poignantly.

This singular memory stands out in my lifetime as one of the few moments I knew...**God was speaking to me**.

Immediately, I sensed an entirely new wave of dedication coming over me. I had been a stay-at-home mom, and I had always taken my job seriously. I loved my job as a wife and mother! But this revelation had me convinced that I must not only be serious about my job as a mother, but also about growing into a better woman...the kind of woman I wanted my daughters to become.

Instantly, the enemy assaulted me with memories of all my failings.

Mistakes.

Missteps.

Insecurities.

As I sat down in one of the tiny school chairs at the little teaching table, tears and fear began to envelop me. Thankfully, it was naptime and the children were all either asleep or resting quietly. I had time to go to the one place I could find strength...**God's Word**.

Unfortunately, I can't recall what Scriptures I read that afternoon, but I do remember the strength I walked away with. Instead of feeling incapable, I had hope welling up inside. Where there had been *fear*, it was overshadowed by *purpose*. I may not have been exactly the type of woman I hoped my daughters would grow up to be at that moment, but I trusted in a God who was not finished with me yet, and I knew He was going to continue His work in me.

And after all, His grace was sufficient.

Parents, your God-given calling to raise up amazing children takes *dedication.*

Focus.

Faith.

Hope.

Lots of love, and oceans of *grace.*

Discipline...mostly *self-discipline!*

There has to come a moment when you decide...when you draw a line in the sand. A moment when you prioritize everything around the most important factors your children must believe and become as adults...and you set about making yourself into the best example of that you can be.

Forget your past.

Don't even let it haunt you one more minute.

Take hold of who you are in Christ *now,* and dedicate the rest of your life to raising up the world-changing adults that are the wee ones in diapers and gym clothes right under your roof.

Beginning With the End in Mind... and Finishing!

Our American culture is focused so much on winning...*so much on success.* Winning the race, scoring the winning goal, even *winning people to Christ!*

I understand...I love to win.

But there is so much more to life than winning.

Indeed, *before a child ever wins anything*, they will lose at countless attempts.

Learning to walk, they fall down hundreds of times before stringing steps together to run.

Learning to run, they will lose dozens of races before they ever even begin to place near the top.

And surely, each failed attempt can be disheartening. Unless you, as a parent, seize the opportunity to teach them to *learn* from each challenge, point out improvement (no matter how minuscule), and continue to cheer them on even when they are dead last, they may very wrongly conclude that competition is not for them. And that would be a sad miscalculation.

Competition is where the fire of drive begins.

Losing with dignity can be the most satisfying win of all...and let me share a personal experience.

We had suffered a difficult year in 2013. Daly Kay was signed up for the Escape from Alcatraz

17

triathlon race. This race challenges triathletes to swim 1.5 miles in the freezing Pacific from Alcatraz Island to shore, then ride eighteen miles through the hilly San Francisco streets, and finish with an eight-mile run up and down those same hills. To a Florida girl these "hills" seem like mountains the size of Everest! We had just faced several personal challenges including moving and my father's death. For those and many other reasons, Daly Kay had not really been training. David decided to take her anyhow, even though the usually frigid race had been moved from June to March.

MARCH.

In San Francisco.

That's like...*sub-arctic water temperatures.*

Regardless, David and Daly Kay competed. They began the swim, and just as David had vowed, he stayed right next to her. Within the first couple of minutes, he asked her how she was doing. As Daly Kay tried to respond she realized she had gotten so cold that hypothermia was setting in, and she couldn't answer. She thought to herself that the only way to get through it was to keep moving... and so she did.

Flopping one arm in front of the other, they made it across the bay. Years of training came in handy as she willed her body to keep moving despite complete numbness. When she got to the beach and tried to walk, she fell face down into the sand. She attempted again, but her limbs were not responding. Cold beyond belief, she spent over an hour on the beach warming up. Any good time she had made across the bay swimming was now lost.

Most people would have/should have quit.

But since the kids were old enough to understand, we had drilled them with: NEVER QUIT. I DON'T CARE IF YOUR LEG FALLS OFF IN THE RACE, PICK IT UP AND HOP TO THE FINISH.

Never ever, ever, ever, ever quit.

They had witnessed their father's "failed attempt" (where he still finished despite food poisoning at the Ironman World Championships) at Kona. They had countless times come in last because of a flat tire, bike crash, or twisted ankle. Truthfully, my kids have lost many more times than they have won. But they always finish. And so...she didn't quit.

The race officials were closing the beach. She hobbled up the sand still numb in her extremities and shivering. She got to the first transition area. Her dad right next to her, he asked if she wanted to try the bike. She did. She wasn't fast by any means, but one mile at a time, she kept moving just ahead of the meat wagon. (That's slang for the guys picking up the injured and the quitters along the way.) She vowed to stay ahead of that truck. And sure enough, she finished the bike ride. Walking into transition two, she still had an arduous eight-mile run of nothing but hills and a death-defying sand ladder.

She had a right to quit.

She hadn't trained.

She was way underweight.

She had suffered through hypothermia.

But this was the day. The decision.

This was the race she would lose and she could still consider herself a winner and conqueror forevermore.

This one decision would be the mile marker from adolescence to womanhood.

The eight-mile run and sand ladder didn't get the best of her either. If you look at the race results, you won't see her name, because she completed the race after the allotted time frame (of course, due to the one hour of warming up on the beach!). But make no mistake, she completed the course. She finished the race.

In my book, she is a winner for that epic loss more so than if she had placed on the podium. *She lost royally*, but she won so much more. That is what years of competition, losing, and occasionally winning will do for a child. It will forge inside of them a spirit of perseverance, endurance, and inner fortitude.

That Alcatraz experience will be something Daly Kay will draw on for the rest of her life. The physical hardship made her more mentally, emotionally, and spiritually disciplined in ways that I am not so sure happen easily outside of competition. A lifetime of hearing "NEVER GIVE UP" pushed her far beyond what everyone else in the meat wagon that day (all of whom were better athletes and far better trained) could give. And that's the best lesson losing can ever teach us.

And the following year? Daly Kay not only completed Alcatraz ahead of the meat wagon, she *won* her age group. The past year's loss stoked the flames of fire in her spirit to not only complete the course, but *compete.*

She may have royally *lost* that first year, but by completing the course, it was the most dignified finish of all. And now, she is Queen of the Rock.

I share this story about Daly Kay because beginning with the end in mind means we have to decide ahead of time that no matter how adverse the circumstances are in our parenting, we won't give up. We will not quit. We may be like Daly Kay at that first Alcatraz competition: unprepared, stumbling, and frigid. We can be unsure of our next step, but we have to trust the Lord and just keep putting one foot in front of the other. We will make mistakes, but we will learn through them and be overcomers. Begin with the end in mind... and finish the race!

2.

The Purpose Path

But indeed for this purpose I have raised you up,
that I may show My power in you, and that My
name may be declared in all the earth.

Exodus 9:16 NKJV

I'd be lying to you if I told you raising kids was easy.

Having a simple strategy to raising a child, like knowing what the finished product is supposed to look like, helps us to begin with the end in mind. But please, never confuse simple with easy. When I say simple, it refers to simple in action or strategy, but does not ever imply that it will be easy.

Ryli, at eighteen years old, is my second oldest. It should make you laugh that I originally trembled with trepidation before her arrival in 1996. I was overcome with fear that I could never love another child the way I loved my first born Daly

Kay. I remember a conversation I had with my now lifelong friend Debbie a few weeks into my pregnancy as I was scared to death about how I could possibly love two children enough! I was convinced there was only room in my heart for one. How could I divide my affections appropriately? Silly me. I learned that adding to my family does not cause my love to divide, but to multiply exponentially. That's just about the only kind of math I'm any good at.

Ryli was born after a long struggle with Intrauterine Growth Retardation, whereby her head was measuring several weeks behind normal growth patterns, but all of her extremities below the neck were *well behind* what was considered acceptable. In my concern for what she could possibly struggle with in her cognitive development as a result of such health challenges, I reached out to my dearest high school friend's mother, Liz. Liz sat with me on the phone as I cried and poured out my heart to her that was full of fear. She prayed in response and negated all my concern. Liz prayed that Ryli would be a picture of health, an absolute genius of a child, who would go on to change the world despite this difficult start in life. In my heart I took Liz's words as the gospel and held on tightly to them as Ryli's debut drew near.

Her health was monitored closely for the last few months and many times we spent nights in the hospital or all-nighters at home trying to stop or slow down contractions. We were overjoyed when she was born only two weeks early and weighing significantly more than the doctors had anticipated at five and a half pounds. Since her head was abnormally bigger in proportion to the rest of her body, we lovingly referred to her as *our little alien*. She began to grow and thrive right away and we were so blessed to finally discover that she had not suffered any long-term effects from such a challenging pregnancy. Liz's prayers had been answered, and we began to enjoy our precious new daughter.

When she was three, Ryli declared she wanted to be a missionary. She loved to read all about these heroes of faith and could recite their harrowing tales of mystery and adventure. At four years old, more evidence of Liz's prayers were coming to fruition as she could read on a middle and high school level and enjoyed thick books like *Watership Down, Tales of Uncle Remus*, and *The Adventures of Peter Cottontail*. You can probably guess that her favorite animals were bunnies. She even sprinkled glitter on herself one night and expected to wake up a rabbit. Easter bunny ears, socks on her hands, and nose a-twitchin' she tried to convince us that her transformation had been completed by a fairy overnight. God, I loved this little character!

But by six years of age, her growth had stalled and she weighed only twenty-eight pounds. Short and skinny, she would eat endlessly and still continue to fall behind on the growth charts. One early morning as I made coffee while getting ready to start the day, she stumbled into the kitchen and collapsed. I rushed her to the hospital to begin what was a several month process between our local St. Mary's Hospital, Miami Children's Hospital, and eventually John's Hopkins Hospital in Maryland. We discovered that Ryli's metabolism worked way too fast and we had to be proactive in tricking her body. But all those hospital stays had begun a love of medicine in her little heart and while we made our rounds, hospital to hospital, Ryli would often beg that I take her room to room so that she could make friends and encourage the other children. Medical missions became her focus by age seven.

Since finishing high school, she's started college, visited Africa, served in a Haitian medical clinic, and volunteers at our local children's hospital. She has become a gifted leader of children and she's the family comedienne. As I share with you a bit about the Purpose Path and apply parts of Ryli's story, I hope to give you a clear understanding of what I've learned over the last twenty years and how Ryli's story is such a poignant example of this process.

Before we begin, I'd like to define the terms we will be using. There won't be a quiz at the end of the chapter, but the outcome of the test could not be more imperative. As a parent, being able to understand and work with these terms will give you immense satisfaction as you have the joyous opportunity to "train up a child in the way he should go." (Proverbs 22:6 ESV) Trust me, there is no greater joy than seeing your child walking toward what they were created to do.

Purpose

All of us were created with a common purpose… to glorify God. This fancy term really just means that our lives will make those around us want to know this God we believe in. Our joy and boldness, even in light of less than perfect circumstances, will make our neighbors, our co-workers, and our acquaintances attracted to Him. This is the answer to why any of us exists in the first place.

We all have the same purpose, to glorify God, but our greatest joy can be found in how we fulfill our purpose by living out our calling.

Calling

Our calling is how God chooses to use us to accomplish our purpose. A calling is not a job. Let me explain the difference...

My purpose is to know God and make God known, to glorify Him. My calling is to raise my children, and to encourage and help other parents do the same. Now, my job is far less glamorous. I change diapers, wipe snot, cart them from football games to doctor's appointments to friends' houses. My job includes everything from the care and keeping of this larger-than-average-size brood, through their college education, and loving them right on into eternity.

When trying to understand your child's *purpose* and *calling* and how that may manifest into a vocation or *job*, we parents have to learn to discern between the determining factors I define below, while leaving wide swaths of possibility open for God to bring us to the place where we begin to understand this enigma. The determining factors below are defined based on my personal experience, but I have found them to be spot-on time and time again.

Strengths & Weaknesses

A child may naturally display different strengths or weaknesses. One child may be able to speak up for themselves easily. Another may have to be taught how to defend themselves or their viewpoint over time.

One child may be born physically more powerful, another may need help to develop ample strength.

One daughter may be completely competitive, while another could care less who wins the game. We may have a child who is academically very strong, and we may have another who struggles with their education. Being careful not to label a child, as a parent we must discern and consider these, as well as many other types of strengths and weaknesses, when trying to navigate through the Purpose Path. Even as you read this I want you to begin to identify and write down what you know about your child already. Whatever pops into your head, *write it down*:

_____

_____

_____

_____

_____

_____

_____

Ability

Where strengths and weaknesses have to do more specifically with character issues, abilities have more to do with a child's *skill* set. You may see that your child has an ability to read people easily. Your child may have good hand-eye coordination that they enjoy participating in sports with. They may have a natural ability with words or communication.

Discerning abilities is a key part of deciphering your child's purpose. Lots of times moms and dads can identify abilities easily, and where they may fail, a teacher or a coach can give them clues. Listen carefully to the things people like to tell you about your child. Write those down too:

_____

_____

_____

_____

_____

Quirks

A child who has a strong competitive desire, an innate strength in academics, and yet is not the most athletic or physically imposing, may be someone who is bound to compete with his brain instead of his brawn. That's not to say that his brawn *cannot* or *should not* be developed. I'm just showing you how some of these unlikely pairings can fit together to make a beautiful finished puzzle. Separately these pieces seem to not fit, but when put together *with prayer* these quirks can add up to something amazing! List some of your child's quirks:

_____

_____

_____

_____

_____

Interests/Hobbies

These are the peripheral enjoyments of the child. Not every kid who loves baseball is meant to go into the major leagues, and yet just because you don't think it's junior's calling to reach and influence masses of people by playing in America's favorite pastime, does not mean that he can't enjoy the game. He can learn the many valuable lessons that come with being a part of the team. Interests and hobbies are healthy additions to your child's life and well worth spending time together doing.

Sometimes an interest or a hobby can be a piece of a puzzle. Sometimes it develops further into a full-blown career. But let's also remember that while we take this business of raising up children seriously, sometimes we just need to spend an afternoon building model airplanes together. What are your child's interests and hobbies?

_____

_____

_____

_____

_____

Passions

Children can be passionate about many things when they are little. They are passionate about their special blankie, passionate about not wanting to leave the park, passionate about French fries. (OK, confession time—that last one I never outgrew.) But as a child grows, you may see them begin to develop a passion for a specific subject, sport, or an interest of a certain kind. They begin to choose books consistently covering that subject. They look for news articles, watch television shows about it, and begin to want to discuss their passion with you *all the time*. Passions can take time to develop, but once they have been birthed it is usually quite difficult to dispel them. Kids tend to come and go with different likes and dislikes but *passions remain*.

For example, Ryli tends to follow trends and enjoy some new fad easily, but her missional mindset of healing and teaching children, enjoying them as she ministers to them, has never waivered. I would now easily say that her passion is teaching, encouraging, and evangelizing to children. Passions can develop at all different ages, so don't be alarmed if your four-year-old has not as of yet declared his undying love for the arts...hang in there, parents. You've got time on your side. List some of your child's passions:

_____

_____

_____

_____

_____

_____

Talent

Some children are born with a natural talent. This goes beyond ability. This talent sticks out when compared with peers who have been in the same form of training or classroom. The best example of talent happens when I compare my two children Daly Kay and Kemper, our fourth daughter. Daly Kay has a passion for sports and absolutely LOVES triathlons and especially swimming, but I would be lying to you if I said she was born *naturally talented*. Every ounce of headway Daly Kay has made in athletics has happened out of pure love of the sport, hard grit, and determination. She was not given beautiful form in any one of the sports disciplines of triathlon, yet she has excelled in them all through her passion and determination. She was not born talented, but she has definitely become so. Kemper, on the other hand, was *born* talented. As a young child, she won many of her swim meets and her triathlons with little to no training.

What are your child's talents?

_____

_____

_____

_____

_____

Giftedness

We like to throw the word *gifted* around a lot as parents, but the truth is there are very, very, VERY few children who are born *gifted*. The cold hard facts are that likely, before anyone ever labels a child as gifted, they have put countless unseen hours into grinding out that talent in hard work and an effort to become better and eventually excel. *Giftedness* is born out of talent, passion, and a lot of hard work.

It's time to brag! What are your child's gifts?

_____

_____

_____

_____

_____

Now that I have defined some of these terms, I can teach you about the Purpose Path that will help guide you through the maze of decisions you as a parent will face. I'll use Ryli as an example to show you how these puzzle pieces fit together.

Ryli's **purpose** is to glorify God. Her **calling** is to bring people the gospel through medical missions work. Her **strength** of seeing the best in everyone belies a missionary's heart. She has a great sense of humor that engages people easily

35

and especially reaches children. Ryli also never gives up on anyone or anything, no matter how challenging or dim a prospect might be. This too will serve her well on the mission field. Her **weaknesses,** which include an occasional lack of personal discernment or judgment, make it actually a benefit in that she reaches out equally to everyone regardless of what most people see on the outside. She has the **ability** to communicate love easily in her eyes and has great empathy for others. Ryli also has an incredible **ability** to help when our children are sick. When our family is ill she keeps records of who has which symptoms and when they were last given medication. Ryli's **quirks** include a high pain tolerance and an absolutely disarming sense of humor. Both of which will no doubt come in handy as she serves the less fortunate. Ryli's **interests** and **hobbies** include long-distance running, which surely developed her endurance, not only physically, but mentally and spiritually. She is also an avid birder and lover of all things natural. Ryli has also begun a rudimentary understanding of natural and homeopathic remedies in case her future missions take her into the bush. But all of these things blend perfectly into her real **passion,** which is to see others renewed and transformed by the loving grace of Jesus.

Ryli graduated from high school and we took her on a medical missions trip to Haiti. While there she served side by side with a team of doctors, medical school students, nurses, and friends her age. The team set up a clinic inside a small Catholic church and saw over 1600 patients in four days. Ryli declared that one week in June in Haiti was the best "vacation" of her life! She derived more joy out of serving and helping to heal the poorest of the poor in the hottest of heat for that week, than she had every other trip our family had taken. Purpose is powerful, folks. As she witnessed compound fractures, gangrenous infections, and necrotic wounds, she found confidence in her calling and comfort in her purpose.

Her desire to heal people, inside and out, is what motivates her on days where she is struggling or being challenged in school. And this, my dear friends, is where the Purpose Path can literally save your teenager from despair and peer pressure. Knowing who they are and why God put them here is your first line of defense against a world that glistens with the fool's gold of idleness and false prosperity.

3.

How to Discover God's Calling for Your Child

For the gifts and the calling of God
are irrevocable.

Romans 11:29 NKJV

Baby Ryli was just three months old. She had finally begun to sleep well and her 5:00 to 8:00 p.m. nightly cry-fest was over and done with. I still hadn't had a period, but I didn't really think too much of it until my friend Debbie said we should just stop off and get a pregnancy test "for fun." Fifteen minutes later, I emerged from my bathroom in shock. Another Reback was on the way.

Soon after, we discovered this would be our third daughter. When friends and family heard the news, most felt disappointed for us. They were sure that the only reason anyone would want to have three babies in less than three years was to get at least one of each sex and be done with the whole process of procreation.

Oh, how wrong they were.

The comments became almost insulting... like who would actually WANT three daughters? Three young'uns in diapers. Three girls getting their periods. Three teenage females under the same roof. Three weddings to pay for. In their minds, what a sad fate the stars had dealt us. It began to really tick me off.

When the search for names began, I thought which name would let the world know we were HAPPY to have another girl? And that's when I landed on Bliss.

However, David thought it sounded like a flower child. My dad snarkily replied, "What's going to be the middle name? 'Fully'?" But no one could give me any better suggestions.

One night I awoke at 2:00 a.m. The baby was due in three weeks and I was desperate for a moniker. As David lay there snoring away, I kept tossing and turning. We had moved into a tiny 600 square foot apartment while we built a new home, so it wasn't like there was somewhere I could go to escape his log-sawing. Finally, I decided if I was awake, he should be, too.

"What's the name going to be? You said you don't like the name Bliss, but you haven't given me any other ideas!" Groggily, he admitted he had no other names in mind, but at least the snoring had stopped. I suggested we pray about it and after a speedy "amen" he was drifting off again. I quickly closed my eyes, hoping the sandman would come to me first, so that I would miss his second chorus of snores. Sleep came, and the next day dawned in our tiny home.

Somewhere near dinnertime, David waltzed in the door. A stack of mail in one hand, he held out a letter to me with the other. He simply said, "You win."

The letter came to our rental home's address for Thomas Bliss. That was it! Her name was decided. Mistaken address or *sign from God*, I was thrilled either way. I was happy to be having my third girl!

The name fit her perfectly. Compared to Daly Kay, who would cry and throw fits so hard she would pass out, and Ryli who would just squawk for three hours nightly as a newborn, this baby was a dream. She never cried. And the first real tears she gave us, at around eighteen months old, even sounded like laughter.

41

By the age of two, Bliss had become quite shy. No one who knows her today ever believes me when I say this, but it was a real challenge to get her out from behind my skirts and to look people in the eye and speak up. For nearly two years, we worked tirelessly to teach her how to use her voice, look directly at others when speaking to them, and stick up for herself. At the age of five, David and I heard her in her bedroom swooshing and jumping on the bed. We peeked in, and there she was doing some version of a Karate Kid move. We asked her what she was doing and she replied, "This is the 1-2-3 Bliss Kapow!"

Gone was the shy girl. She had found new purpose in defending her seemingly helpless older sister Ryli, who still fancied herself a bunny rabbit. Any time some kid denied the absolute truth of the Easter bunny and made Ryli cry, they got the 1-2-3 Bliss Kapow. Wanna go toe-to-toe and tell Bliss that her American girl doll isn't real and doesn't have feelings? 1-2-3 Bliss Kapow. At swim team, the gang of kids thought she was terrific. She raced and played hide-and-seek in the saw grass and kids loved trying to outsmart her with their witty remarks. My beautiful Bliss was such a tomboy and could climb trees quick as a whip and did it all the while wearing her little Lilly Pulitzer dresses and ruffled monogrammed bloomers. Life was good. All the effort in teaching her to speak up and speak out had really transformed her into quite a little leader.

As Bliss grew, Daddy's favorite pastime with the girls was to watch movies. David was never much of a reader. He would take them to see Disney films at the theaters over and over, and re-watch our favorite family classics like *Mulan* endlessly. Because it was something Daddy would do with them, movie-watching held special value and memories. For such an active, busy family, I warred with myself many times about the prudence of her "wasting" so much time in front of a television. If she wasn't watching a movie, she was hidden off in a corner somewhere buried deep in a book. She had learned how to spin a good yarn and over the years she became increasingly more talented in her artwork. Her drawing went from stick figures to incredible dimension as she often absconded with an instructional drawing book and a sketchpad. As a result, Bliss became quite a storyteller.

When Bliss was just eight years old, we adopted our son, Courson. The first time Bliss walked into the NICU and saw all the tiny babies, she declared emphatically that she wanted to become a nurse and help children. She began to sing and croon over this newest addition to our family and her voice soothed him immensely. A heart for orphans was born.

While she originally planned to become a nurse in the NICU, as her love for storytelling, film, and art grew, she began to also write children's stories, epic screenplays, and became quite a conceptual artist. She could look at an outfit, a room, or a film and tell you visually why it did or didn't work and plot-wise what was missing or what was spectacular. Her special dates for her birthdays became movie marathons where we would sit in a theater for hours on end watching back-to-back films. Popcorn, Coke, and spiral notebook in hand she would analyze each scene.

Also, unbeknownst to me, she had been secretly singing in the pantry and recording herself, working on her vocal training. All this to say that Bliss's abilities, talents, passions, and giftedness have led her to pursue a career in the film industry. Continuously developing creative content, critiquing films, and practicing her voice consistently convinced us that it was well worth the effort on her behalf to participate in local plays, allow her to produce short films, and invest in proper equipment, as well as find a voice coach that could continue to train her.

It hasn't always been a straight and narrow path to determine what Bliss's calling or vocation would be, but over the years the field in which she should spend the bulk of her time became more obvious. Her passion was more than convincing!

When Bliss was a baby, we began with the same basic guidelines we always do. Solid *spiritual* foundation. Good *education*. We knew shyness wouldn't help her accomplish her goals, so we set out to deter that and instead teach her personal confidence.

Bliss always loved stories about women who were tough gals. Ladies who never took no for an answer became her favorite characters. Gladys Aylward traveling through the snow-capped mountains of China with over a hundred orphans in tow. Joan of Arc, young and leading an army in transforming her nation, misunderstood and martyred. Mulan, fighting in her father's stead and for her country, never letting her femininity stop her from protecting that which she loved and honored. Erin Brockovich, the unlikely underdog with enough heart and grit to break all the wrong rules for the right reasons.

Because of her little brother Courson, when she declared a special place in her heart for orphans, we thought it was beautiful. That determination has her working diligently through school and in her purpose she is focused.

I share all this with you about Bliss growing up so that you can see how her name, her joy, her personality, and her passions have led us to a place where we can now see how strong her self-generated initiative is and how it is firmly based on her passion and drive. Biographies, books, and films had shown her who she wanted to become, and now she wanted to do the same for other little girls and boys. Bliss will eventually use her influence in the film industry to help orphans out of poverty and into the loving arms of a forever family. Suddenly all those hours in front of the TV were guilt free as far as I was concerned!

The Bliss Factor

After such a shy start in life, it is funny to see how she became such a strong-willed young lady. By the time she was five years old, not a single Sunday school teacher liked her. They'd complain that she argued with them, bossed other kids around, and after observing discreetly from the sidelines, it was easy to see why. Bliss had a knack for finding the underdog, defending the less "popular" and calling a teacher out on favoritism. As a young girl, she didn't even realize what she was doing, but as she matured, we came to call this litmus test the "Bliss Factor." She could logically defend her arguments, and when confronted with injustice, her emotions ran high. She would admit when she was wrong, but if she knew she was right, she would become entrenched. When parents come to me lamenting about their strong-willed child, I gladly point them toward Bliss and defy their complaints with the fact that a strong-willed child is a brilliant leader in the making. Parents just have to make sure they train that child to lead others in the *right* direction.

I once read in a book that girls want to be seen as beautiful and adored, while boys like to be known as strong, courageous, and well-respected. I gagged. Having ten daughters, I thought to myself that if I only raised girls who desire to be known as beautiful and adored, I had failed as a mother. You can get that kind of reaction from simply viewing a stone statue or a piece of art. If I raised my five sons to actually like girls that only thought this way, I will have utterly fallen short. This sad, shortsighted, over-simplification of femininity was not what I had in mind for my daughters. In light of Bliss's story, I hope you are inspired to strive for far more in raising up lady leaders who can inspire, define, and dignify their generation.

Embrace your strong-willed child. Make sure they know their purpose and how to accomplish it through their calling. Develop their strengths and train their weaknesses. Through hard work, give them opportunities to explore their abilities, talents, interests, and hobbies. When their passion comes, let it ignite their world and light their way through those difficult struggles that the teenage years can bring. Many times, Bliss's passion for her future makes today's choices easy in light of all she wants to accomplish. Today's temptations have far less pull with so much hope and promise in the future.

How the Purpose Path Looks Different for Each Child

Bliss's purpose path took a very different route than that of both sisters before her and all of her siblings to follow her. Bliss needed room to find her own way. It took encouragement and support from both her parents to pursue her true passions, God's strength (and a little of mom's nudging) to overcome her shyness, and her own wisdom to recognize her innate courage and leadership qualities. The Purpose Path, as we've come to call it, can give you a place to start with each of your children, no matter where you are in your parenting journey.

At the beginning of the path is the very most basic guidelines or goals you have in mind for your child. These can include but are certainly not limited to:

- An Education: elementary, secondary, collegiate, graduate
- Healthy Lifestyle: athletics, nutrition, soundness of mind
- Spiritual: knows God, understands salvation, knows where to get wisdom and answers
- Financially Independent: Hard-working and able to take care of themselves and their family

But these are just some of the baselines. Your baselines may be different than mine and that's fine. It's important to establish what the bare minimums are in your list of priorities. The beauty of this idea is that whether your child is a week old, a year old, or ten to fifteen years old, you can begin with a baseline and always work your way up from there. It is never too late. Establish goals, begin to implement a plan to incorporate them into your lifestyle, and walk toward making them a reality with your child.

You have your baselines, and as your child ages, you will notice certain aptitudes, interests, capabilities, and talent or giftedness, so keep a log. Look at the puzzle pieces and see how they fit into or add to the baseline. I have a legal pad for each child and keep track of different things I notice about each one. Date the events, the comments people make, the amazing things you notice. My notes also include funny quirks, silly sayings, and interesting things others have noticed about my child. Maybe these talents become part of who or what your child will grow into, they may be part of his or her calling. As your child develops, as you walk in encouraging their capabilities, honestly evaluating their weaknesses and how these specific traits can be used for a purpose and in a calling, you begin to see the path a bit more clearly. Things are starting to narrow.

Listen to teachers and coaches, as well as others involved and invested in your child's life. In your child's education, as you see him taking an interest or developing a passion for certain things, the path becomes narrower and narrower. All factors begin to point a certain direction. You will be able to make decisions for education, athletics, schedules, and so forth based on what has become a more obvious anointing on their life.

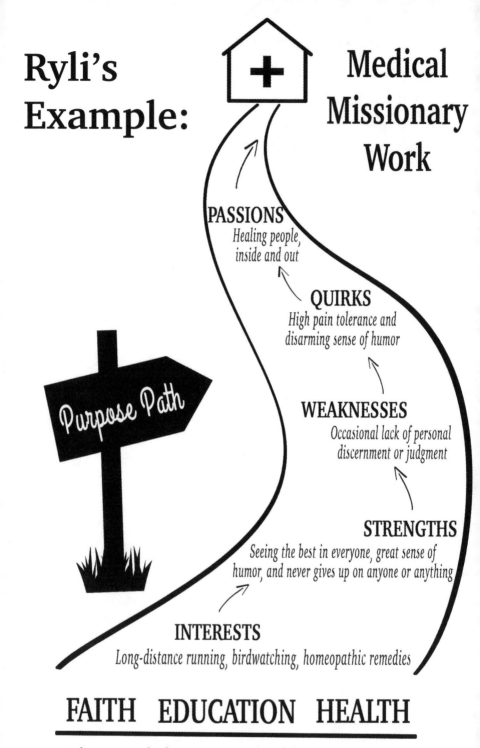

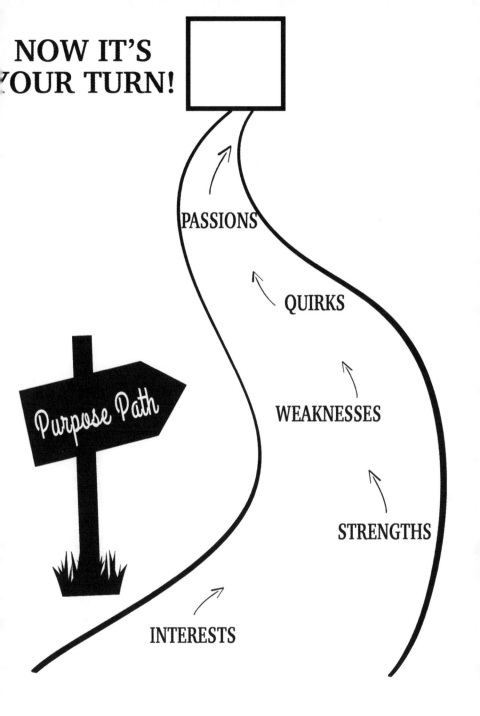

NOW IT'S YOUR TURN!

PASSIONS

QUIRKS

WEAKNESSES

Purpose Path

STRENGTHS

INTERESTS

List your family's basic guidelines and priorities above!

4.

Feeling Overwhelmed? Overcome!

From the end of the earth I will cry to You,
When my heart is overwhelmed;
Lead me to the rock that is higher than I.
Psalm 61:2 NKJV

Trust me, as a mother of fifteen, I know just a little bit about feeling overwhelmed. I wasn't always a mom to such a large tribe. I started off with one child...and that was overwhelming. And when my second baby was born, I thought surely I couldn't possibly handle more than two children. After Bliss was born, I threw my hands up in the air one morning when she was just a few weeks old and all three of them were crying and emphatically stated, "I'm doing the best I can! Two of you are going to have to wait!" Whether you have one child or a dozen, I can understand and completely relate when a parent says they are overwhelmed.

I want you to know these bits of wisdom I am sharing with you come from hard won battles in my mind, through countless mistakes and misgivings in raising my family, and many, many cups of coffee and hours spent in prayer. None of this came easy to me...but I'll gladly have taken the bumps and bruises along the way if it means other parents can learn from them.

The sheer scope and sequence of raising a child is just so...**overwhelming**. We get the baby sleeping through the night, and they figure out how to roll over. Now they cry because they are stuck on their belly. We get baby to be happy sleeping in *any* position, and then, they figure out how to stand up in their crib, and now they can't get down. We get junior to stop complaining about the meal he is served, but he still eats like he's chewing his cud. We get dear daughter to work on her math skills, but her selfishness is just *mind* boggling.

It's always sumthin' folks. Always sumthin'.

And when we look at all we have to work on, day in and day out, it can be *disheartening*. A coach tells us our son was lazy at practice, we receive an email from a teacher about our daughter's attitude, and then our mother-in-law complains that she didn't get a thank you note for the birthday gift.

Really?

Folks, we have to remember in those moments of sheer panic, how far we have come. Remember last year when junior would barely get out of the car for practice? We know our daughter struggles with shyness, but she has made progress! Some days the victories are small, but they are never insignificant. For months at a time we may feel like we are losing ground, **but we must never give up.** And regardless, we must *never* characterize or describe our child by their sins or shortcomings, lest we perpetuate the very problem we are trying to eradicate. Our son will never be a "good student" if we keep describing him as someone who struggles in school. Dear daughter will never speak respectfully if we keep telling everyone what a handful she is and how she has such a smart mouth.

When we are drowning in our parenting to-do list, we should recall how God has given us wisdom to handle other challenges, and He will give us the strength and know-how to handle today as well. Without this perspective, I would have surely gone mad over a decade ago.

Over the years, this verse has brought me great

comfort:

"If you need wisdom, ask our generous God, and he will give it to you." (James 1:5 NLT)

The Lord wants us to know that He will give us wisdom and He won't get onto us for our past failures and mistakes. He is eager to help. God is not a miser with His answers, He gives wisdom generously. When we are overwhelmed with the uncertainty of our circumstances and don't know what to do, He can overwhelm us with His love, grace and understanding. He has been more than generous with me over the last twenty years!

How to Overcome Being Overwhelmed

I love *The Message* translation of the Bible I have been using recently! It is bringing old familiar Scriptures into a fresh light and really encouraging me in my faith. This next Scripture is another one that has brought me so much encouragement when I feel overcome with the responsibility of parenting:

> *This is a large work I have called you into, but don't be overwhelmed by it. It's best to start small. Give a cool cup of water to someone who is thirsty, for instance. The smallest*

*act of giving or receiving makes you
a true apprentice. You won't miss
out on a thing.* (Matthew 10:40-42
MSG)

I remember when I was pregnant with baby
number four. While in the womb, Kemper could
kick my groin area so hard it would truly make my
knees buckle. She had bruised my ribs. This child
was by far one of my toughest pregnancies.

One night I just cried to David from the pain
and pressure she was putting on my lower abdo-
men and swore I would never again have another
baby. He said for me to stop it, the baby could hear
what I was saying and I could be hurting her feelings. "What about MY FEELINGS?" I yelled back at
him. That was the last time he ever tried that tactic as a consolation, *bless his heart.*

Daly Kay was in kindergarten, Ryli was in a
little preschool a couple mornings a week, and
Bliss was a wee whirly dervish that I had a tough
time keeping up with for those few hours we had
alone. One particular morning, I had settled Bliss
in front of a *Veggie Tales* video while I went to go
switch the laundry loads around. As I was leaning
over the machines, Kemper delivered one of her
best roundhouse kicks and I fell to the floor. After
the pain subsided, I just began to weep.

The sheer overwhelmingness of starting over with a newborn, who was obviously bent on my destruction, just did me in. I couldn't bear the thought of breastfeeding with my inevitable cracked and bleeding nipples. No sleep. School *and* teachers *and* homework *and* sports. Ryli's preschool teacher kept reminding me what a problem she was in the classroom. David's work schedule was such that we barely saw him. And that stupid blinking *Veggie Tales* song blaring from the living room was driving me crazy. My back against the dryer, I sat like a rag doll, weeping until I heard the end of the video.

I wish I had known this verse at that time. *I just needed to focus on making lunch*...not how I was going to deal with breastfeeding in a month. I only had to make it to naptime. I needed to remember that even though the prospect of raising one child, or four, or fifteen is completely overwhelming at any given moment, the job AT HAND is not.

If you find yourself feeling overwhelmed, just focus on the next duty. The one right in front of you.

Have a cool cup of water. Be refreshed in the Lord and know that He will send what you need, when you need it. It is a large work, but be willing to give encouragement to others and receive refreshment, encouragement, and instruction along the way from someone a little bit further down the road than you...someone like me.

So if you are feeling overwhelmed, please know that it happens to all of us. The best advice I can give you is to focus on what is right at hand, and trust that He will send refreshment and encouragement to you in your parenting marathon. The smallest act of giving (*and as a parent, doesn't that completely characterize our work?*) or receiving is what makes us a disciple of Christ. The moment by moment decisions to focus on the task at hand makes us a follower and a disciple of the One who is refreshment and strength.

Even though I spent the first three chapters teaching you how to look ahead, to be a visionary parent, to begin with the end in mind, and to look for purpose and develop a plan, if we ONLY look ahead, we will become inundated, engulfed, and overwhelmed.

It's a lot like driving a car cross-country. For the sake of fun, let's pretend to take my ideal road trip of traveling Route 66 in a vintage Chevy. Route 66 was one of the first highways to go state-to-state. This monumental roadway began in Chicago, Illinois and made its way through eight states to the western terminus of Santa Monica, California. I've always wanted to drive what sections of this historic route remain intact, ideally in a vintage automobile!

Figuratively, as parents, we have a map to tell us where we are going (purpose, plan, vision), but we can only see the road right in front of us (the next task: making lunch, finishing homework). We have to spend time looking over our map and developing our strategy to parent effectively, but if we *only* look at the map, we won't be driving anywhere. If we just look at the next job (naptime, ballet practice) we could be circling the block for decades. Parenting is a long haul. We have to stop from time to time, review our map and make sure we are still headed toward our intended destination of Santa Monica.

Eventually, on that fateful day in my laundry room, I came back from the brink of emotional overload with little Kempies in my womb and went on to have many more babies and even adopt a few. We laughed when Kemper was born because as soon as she came out she was kicking and screaming like crazy. Long and lanky, she got a perfect Apgar score and my obstetrician admitted she had never witnessed a baby who was that physically strong from the first moment of life. *Figures.*

Kemper was a name we actually had chosen before we knew it would be a girl. She was named after our close friend and Olympic triathlete Hunter Kemper. David had competed in the Kona Ironman World Championships that year, so we named her after a triathlete to also commemorate David's lifelong goal and accomplishment. Little did I know that name would impart such strength into her little being!

Being overwhelmed is a common emotion in parenthood. Over the last twenty years of parenting fifteen kids, I have learned that routine, priorities, and vision (along with a good nap or a decent night's sleep) can pull us back to sanity and bring us stability. Keeping our hands busy with the job right in front of us will stop our emotions from getting the best of us. Anxiety and fear can rob us of all the joy in parenting, and they usually come circling when my mind is busy but my hands are not. *Just keep at it,* moms and dads.

Parenting As an Endurance Sport

I have learned a lot by marrying into an athletic family and since Kemper is such a fine young athlete, competing alongside her has been a real joy. I've made a tradition the last four years out of running the Disney Princess half marathon with my oldest children. The time away with the big kids is priceless and the physical exertion is small compared to the fun we have training together.

But this year, a thought dawned on me: *Parenting is not a sprint.* It's an ultramarathon.

The parents that brag how early their baby is crawling or walking, how many words their baby knows, how many languages their toddler can speak, or how fast their middle-schooler runs can drive us all crazy. Those things are great, and even exciting, I will admit. But these small successes pale in comparison to the long-term goal of raising an amazing adult. We get the idea from these braggadocios moms and dads that parenting is graded by their kid's performance. If our child's accomplishments don't stack up to the kinds of hoops their child can jump through, then we stink as a parent...and worse, *our kid stinks, too.*

I'm going to go out on a limb here and say that I don't know exactly when we can gauge our parenting as a success, but it certainly isn't by two years old, and it definitely isn't by middle school. Sure, our children at those stages may be "performing well" outwardly, but what's on the inside may not be so apparent. We will only know if our child's "performance" is for real when their heart attitudes include serving those around them on their own initiative, loving and empathizing with others, and when they make character choices that are wise, but not always *easy*. These types of measurements simply cannot be made at such an early age. Honestly, values and virtues can take a decade or two to get inside of the child.

Which brings us back to my ultramarathon analogy.

If you've ever competed in a running race of any kind, you'll instantly get what I am saying. Hundreds of runners line up at the start. The gun goes off and BLAM! *Forty-seven people take off like cheetahs.* The cheetahs are running the first hundred yards like that's all there is to the race...and they putter out pretty fast. Those are the parents hung up on all the insignificant parenting details at an early age—judging their success (and everyone else's too) on things that, in the long run, really don't matter as much as one might think. For example, I have struggled with breastfeeding for over two decades. I wish I could go back and tell my twenty-one-year-old self that it's not so much *what* I feed my baby (breast milk) but how I feed her (with love and affection) that matters. Many such things PALE in comparison to teaching moral heart issues and getting a quality education.

Then you have the people that pace themselves based on someone else's capabilities. These moms and dads are racing away constantly comparing themselves to others instead of focusing on THEIR race, THEIR kids and the specific needs of THEIR family. That gets exhausting, and these folks generally give up trying altogether. They begin to disqualify themselves from their own finish based on someone else's ability. Ridiculous, but easy to fall into.

Finally, you have those strong and steady racers. Folks who ran when they could, walked through the water stops, cruised the downhill, and slowed for the uphills on the course. These parents just kept their eye on the goal—the finish line. They focused on the character traits they want for their children, the type of man or woman they prayed this child would become. They trusted that Jesus—who began this good work in their child—would complete it! Sometimes these racers' pace might have slowed to almost a crawl, but at least they continually kept moving forward.

And eventually...they finish.

This year, Daly Kay, Ryli, Bliss, Kemper, and I completed the 13.1 mile race with power still left in our legs. We had fun singing songs almost the whole course. The girls had lots of good laughs and enjoyed encouraging other runners as we clipped along. We walked the water stops, slowed down on the uphills, and took the time to enjoy one another's company. BUT WE FINISHED...even when we were moving forward slowly.

So remember, parenting is not a sprint. It's an ultramarathon...with long-term goals and far-reaching implications. *Don't* get hung up on a sprint-like mentality that focuses on things that have very little to do with the final outcome of the adult you are raising. *Don't* focus on how someone else is gauging the race. Fix your eyes on the prize of Christ and the finish line of an adult that loves and serves Him.

5.

Don't Raise an Obedient Child

For God has not given us a spirit of fear, but of
power and of love and of a sound mind.

2 Timothy 1:7 NKJV

Glory Grace is our fifth daughter. Tired of the endless gender questions during my pregnancies, we
decided that since we really didn't care whether
we had a boy or a girl, we wouldn't find out until
the baby arrived. Because her birthday was near
Independence Day, I chose Glory as her name.
David agreed, Glory sounded beautiful with Grace.
Funny to note—she is the fifth daughter, both her
first and middle names have five letters in them,
five is the number of grace in the Scriptures, and
this child exudes love and grace in a way that is

extraordinary.

She was one of those rare babies *born* beautiful (as compared to my first four who, like most infants, took time to show their cuteness, *bless their hearts*). Glory Grace is the kind of kid that if born first, parents wonder why everyone else struggles so much with their children. She really is a sweet, sweet child. When she was about fifteen months old, we flew from Florida to Hawaii. As she began to rub her eyes and fuss on the plane I just leaned over, passed her a blankie and told her it was naptime. No joke, Glory grabbed the blankie, leaned her head to one side of the car seat, closed her eyes and went to sleep. I was astounded. She was so easy-going.

But having such an easy-going child also has its challenges. We had to teach her to stand up for herself, and speak up over our louder than average brood. Her polite tendency was to let everyone else speak first, but she soon learned if she waited for everyone to be quiet, she might never get heard! Eventually she grew to retain her sweetness and gained some grit along the way.

By the time she was eleven, Glory had begun wearing a tiara. Her sister Daly Kay had gotten one on her 18th birthday, and Glory thought it was so beautiful that she just had to have one of her own. We noticed when she had the crown on, her normally lovely posture became even straighter. Her quiet voice carried more strength. Glory Grace is who taught me one of my most important parenting lessons to date: Why raising an obedient, rule-following child is just not the goal.

It's funny the things people will ask me when they discover I have fifteen children. Most times, the questions are a barrage of *"How do you do it?"* and *"Don't you know what causes that?"* Sometimes the questions are heartfelt—"How did you get to adopt four children?" or "Why have so many?"

But one of the most important questions that rarely gets asked is: *What's the most important thing I can teach my children*?

Of course the most vital thing to teach any child is the redemptive power that faith in Jesus gives us. But past this, most parents just tend to focus on raising well-behaved kids.

As if being well-behaved is the end-all goal of Christianity. *Be good.* If I have "good" kids then I am a good parent. If my kids know all the rules and follow them then I have done my job. An added bonus may include a college education or an exemplary skill of some sort, but truly it just boils down to their behavior, right?

WRONG.

Look, moms and dads, I can see how we easily fall into this trap...and yes, it's a trap. When the children are small we are basically relegated to making sure the child survives the day—no matter how many times they try and self-destruct between jumping off the couch, climbing out of their crib, and swallowing everything possible to block their windpipe. We begin to think to ourselves that if we could ever just get through a meal at a restaurant without being humiliated, just make it through the grocery store without the three-year-old having a total meltdown, if we could just get them to listen to us and do what we say, we will have DONE IT. Done our jobs. Gotten those little wee beasties tamed and they may even manage to make us, as moms and dads, look pretty good in the process.

I am in no way saying that obedience itself is not important. It is. In fact, your child's life may very well depend on them stopping when you ask them to, thereby avoiding being run over in the street. We must teach our children to listen to us and obey, but this is something that is rarely accomplished completely at a very young age and I have my sneaking suspicions that's why the Good Lord gave us a solid sixteen to twenty years with our children under our wings.

But while my short-term goal may be obedience, I do NOT want an obedient twenty-one-year-old. Instead, I want a young adult who knows the rules and when to break them.

"No fighting in school," may be the rule, but I want a teenager who knows when to stick up for a friend and get a bump or bruise in the process. "Live peaceably with all men," say the Scriptures, but I want my child to know it is all right to not be "peaceable" when someone is trash talking another classmate. Playing to win may be the unspoken rule, but when my child chooses all the class "losers" to be on her team for dodge ball and they get creamed, my child just won at the game of life.

You see, without paying careful attention, we can accidentally raise a child who is just obedient and not resourceful or full of initiative. We could raise a child who knows the rules and not the guiding principles, so they never weigh out which is the greater need. And I have two really good examples of this.

When I was heavily pregnant with my fourth child. I had taken my three daughters, then six, four, and three years old to play on the beach while my friend and I talked. The girls were skimming along in the waves in barely a foot of water when the hair on the back of my neck stood up. Prompted by what I can only describe as a "Holy Warning," I yelled, "GET OUT NOW!" to the children in a voice that screamed terror. The girls sprinted out of the water and ran thirty feet up to the dune. They then turned around and asked, "Why, Mama?"

Thank God they ran before they asked. A tiger shark began rapidly approaching as they sprinted out of the water, and I saw it heading straight for where the girls were playing. Surely, a tragedy had been avoided because they listened quickly. Shaken, I gathered them up and left the beach that day thanking God for their safety. Ever since then, SHARK has been the buzzword we use when someone doesn't listen and obey quickly.

Fast-forward about ten years. A younger cousin is having a surf party at the beach. About twenty-five children are playing in the waves, trying out surfboards, and enjoying a fun day in the ocean. One of the dads, a local surfing legend, pointed to the water and said to me, "Shark. Get the kids out."

In my *do-it-or-else-you'll-be-sorry* voice I promptly told every kid to get out of the water immediately. Out of the twenty-five kids, five decided they would rather play than listen. I explained that there was a shark in the water and those stinkers started arguing with me that because they didn't see it, I was wrong.

And guess who's still in the water between all these five- to eight-year-old arguers? My oldest daughter.

Daly Kay had grown into an incredible swimmer and reasoned that since she was such a strong athlete, she would rather stay in the water and gather up these yahoos to get them out of the ocean rather than leave them in there defenseless. Even as they ignored the clear commands to leave the water, she was pulling them out to safety. She broke the rules. She disobeyed. But she did the greater thing. She had quite possibly saved these kids from their own foolishness.

As our kids age, we must move from merely teaching them simple obedience to focusing on the greater principles. We should transition from rule following and consequences to the challenging arena of coaching them through difficult situations that aren't so easy to discern. I add this part into Glory's story because it is right around her current age of eleven to thirteen that we begin to lead this transition. If not, we risk raising a legalist who can't love others easily because they are too busy keeping the rule tally. It's also quite probable that our child will see through the black and whiteness of our rules and rebel in search of favor, love, and understanding.

My kids aren't perfect and you can be guaranteed that I'm not either. There have been plenty of times that we've had to learn the hard way to obey. But at the end of the journey, I don't just want an obedient adult. I want a faith-filled bold individual that knows the rules and when to break them. I want my children to be so full of His Word, favor, and grace that they walk in confidence knowing their Heavenly Father loves them, and their parents have their back. If we only focus on the short-term goal of teaching our children obedience, rather than the long-term goal of boldness through faith in Christ, we will have missed our opportunity as parents to raise up a generation of world changers.

With a name like Glory Grace you better believe she has taught us a lot about what true grace looks like. Glory would have easily been a rule-follower. But I have realized that if we focus solely on the "do nots" of life, or the Big 10 (commandments) in our rule teaching, we will fall desperately short. Our children will become so consumed with what not to do and judging others by these standards, that fear of doing wrong will be their main focus instead of boldness to do what's right. Children must grow through learning the rules, under-standing the greater principles behind them, and eventually, know when to break the rules. We have to change from telling them what to do, to them knowing why and doing the right thing without being asked. We must teach them to move from being obedient to becoming brave.

My Secret Parenting Weapon

When Glory Grace was born, Daly Kay was seven. We had just begun going to a church that simply preached the Bible...chapter by chapter, verse by verse. One Sunday, the pastor mentioned that the most influential practice in his life was learning to memorize Scripture. He started with just a verse or two per week and eventually trained himself to be able to memorize an entire chapter. As a new homeschooler, I somewhat haphazardly decided that this was going to be a part of my curriculum. I had no way of knowing what a monumental deci-sion this was going to be.

It wasn't easy. A few kiddos went along effort-lessly. I had others, who shall remain nameless, that nearly drove me batty pretending they had not memorized, just to push the envelope on a weekly basis, for months in a row. But, as any good hard-headed-raised-in-the-backwoods-Texan would, I stuck to my guns. And over time, entire chunks of the Good Book were indelibly etched into their hearts.

"Well good for you," you might be thinking. And yes, thank you, it was good for me. As I had them recite it over and over to me all week and every weekend, I began to memorize chunks, too. Over the last twelve years, the girls have memorized the books of Proverbs, Revelations, a gospel of their choosing, and then moved on to other books that mean something to them personally as they have matured in their faith and purpose. And yes, memorizing BOOKS of the Bible makes a huge difference rather than just a verse from here and a verse from there.

But here's the REAL benefit...

As a parent, when we discipline a child, we are working from the outside inward. In other words, we are dealing against their flesh and hoping our efforts are making a difference inwardly, in their spirit.

But when we have them memorizing Scripture, the Holy Spirit is working from the inside out. And that, my friends, makes for a total win. Every time.

I don't have to base my parenting decisions on my "perfection" (or lack thereof). My children have memorized enough about grace and they know my authority in their life is God-given, regardless. I can speak plainly to my children about their present character challenges, and because of the Word hidden in their hearts, the Spirit bears witness inside them that my assessment is correct. As I pray about the different aspects of their training, and I can trust the Spirit, that is the WORD in their hearts, is doing a work I cannot see.

The peace this brings is unsurpassed.

No, the children are not perfect, and certainly, neither am I. But His Word and His Spirit are, and they are doing a work from the inside out that my discipline simply cannot do alone.

Memorizing Scripture is my secret parenting weapon. If you're willing to take up this sword and fight the good fight, then it can be yours too. This secret weapon forges a heart of wisdom and bravery that rules alone could never accomplish.

6.

How I Run This House

...diligence is man's precious possession.
Proverbs 12:27 NKJV

I'll be honest with you, I was raised with a bit of a silver spoon in my mouth. When I was born, my father was struggling to get his third marriage off the ground and his newest business endeavor underway, but both would eventually be successful. As a baby, my mother sewed or crocheted all my clothes because there was no money in the budget for store-bought goods. I distinctly remember having concrete floors and plastic lawn furniture in our family room because carpet and furnishings were too expensive. But by the time I was eight, we had full-time staff in our home. As an only child, these people became like extended family to me and were formative influences in my childhood.

Even though we had a housekeeper and groundskeeper, my father never let me sit on my laurels. We had horses, which meant we also had horse manure to shovel, stables to clean, and other farm animals to feed. We had acres of land, which meant we also had acres of gardening, trail clearing, and fences to mend. It was a glorious upbringing in a small Texas, one-stop-light town. During the summers, my father had a vintage yacht in Vancouver, Canada and we cruised up and down the Pacific Northwest coast. This boat also had no shortage of work to be done. My father, the former United States Marine, made sure I was *well acquainted* with hard work.

As a child, I can't say I admired his tenacity and appreciated his tough training on my behalf. I felt almost bitter. We *had* help...a captain, a first mate...why should I shine the brass? Clean the stainless steel? Scrub the decks? Wash the windows?

Oh! And his incessant need for perfection in a job completed by a nine-year-old would just drive me bonkers! But because of his insistence, by the time I was a teenager, I possessed an iron will, a solid work ethic, and a drive to do things to the best of my ability (no doubt shaped by my father's relentless pursuit of perfection) in all I set my hands to. I didn't realize it then, but he was teaching me *sweat equity.*

You see, while he drove me to diligence, he was simultaneously teaching the value of a dollar and a sense of pride in my work. I didn't yet understand the importance of serving others, but by his constant insistence on a job well done, my father had taught me what good service was. I had my duties to perform, whether at home on the farm or away on the boat. I took good care of the things he bought for me, as I realized he worked hard for that money he spent. When I was nine, he purchased a beautiful wooden rowboat with teak decks and oars as a special Valentine's Day gift for me. I was so very proud of my little vessel. I rowed beach-to-beach, boat-to-boat, washing her daily and shining her brass oar buckles. I loved that little boat, and *I loved the man who bought it for me, too.*

Hard work. Tough standards. Consistent rewards and consequences. These are the foundations I drew upon when it came time to teach my own children. I tried to hold my home and children to the wonderful standards my parents had taught me. Out of respect for my husband and his efforts on our behalf, as well as an honoring tribute to my parents, I always wanted my garden to look nice, my children to look adorable, and our home to be run well. And as long as I had the same kind of help my parents had, I could keep up a pretty good façade.

David had been blessed in his work to the point where we could afford some help in the home. Although strictly there to maintain the household, tensions always arose when they tried to take over my position as mom or question my decisions.

The final straw came when David was overseas.

David was out of town for a triathlon championship; all five of my little girls came down with a virulent stomach bug. By 2:00 a.m., I was also violently throwing up and was reduced to simply covering up the piles of vomit with whatever towels I could find. Sprawled on the floor outside the bedroom of my two oldest daughters, when the maid arrived, I could barely whisper, "Thank God you're here." She took one look around—said, "I quit,"—and walked out.

Ticked beyond all belief that I was even in this position in the first place, I vowed to never again need, require, or hire help. Daly Kay was about eight years old at the time, but I looked at her with all the resolve I could muster between bouts of vomiting and said, "Never again. We will never again rely on anyone else. We can *do* this."

At the time, she agreed with me, her little body weak from an all-nighter with the flu. I'm not so sure she knew exactly what she was agreeing to, but it felt good in my mind to at least have a partner in crime.

Within a few days, when our health and vigor returned, I began to implement a plan. I had absolutely no idea how far reaching it would become. When David arrived home he was shocked to discover the house in order and no one to thank but myself and his eight, six, and five-year-old daughters.

Zone Defense

Lots of times people ask me how I do it. How do I run this household?

The answer is simple. Notice I did not say *easy*. There is nothing *easy* about parenting, running a household, and least of all about raising fifteen children.

The simple answer is that I have different children over different areas of the house—different zones. Trinity, our sixth daughter, at ten years old

85

is responsible for all the laundry. Two of our girls, ages fourteen and twelve, are over all the kitchen duties. There are more than a dozen zones in our house, all clearly divided up, and I rarely shift who is on what job. In other words, if a child is on laundry, they better get cozy because it's likely that laundry will be their job for a year or two.

The reasons I do this are many. First of all, if I were constantly shifting who was in what zone I could easily forget, blame the wrong child, and likely a child could claim ignorance saying he thought so-and-so was still on that job. No siree. The child knows their job, I know their job, and everybody else knows their job because it has been their job for a long time. The child is without excuse for executing their zone properly because they have had time to learn it.

How do I know they learned it?

Because I taught it to them.

Diligently.

I showed them time and again, over the course of several weeks, what a well-executed job/zone looks like, and they saw me sweat and labor to work alongside them and train them. I didn't point from the couch, complain from the TV room, or look halfheartedly over my phone's screen...I stinkin' showed 'em.

Zones are not implemented only because we need the work done. No, no, no! They are far more important than that. Zones are my way of checking on various character traits I am training into the hearts of my children.

- Diligence.
- Follow through.
- Consistency.
- A servant's heart—someone who willingly works and has a joyful attitude about it.

Zones give parents insight into character development. A parent may be passing on the responsibility of the laundry to simply get it done...but that would be short-sighted. We should be passing on the laundry to teach the skill. We want to teach our child to participate in the family, anticipate when someone will need their uniform, keep a running list of necessities like detergent and dryer sheets for the grocery shopper, and serve with love by how they neatly fold towels and lovingly hang mom's favorite dress to drip dry (without the shoulders being misshapen by a child-size hanger...just saying).

Teaching my children about zones has done wonders for their administrative and management skills. It has made them singularly responsible and at the same time completely *other*-oriented. If you decide to utilize zones, teach and train them well, maintain consistent standards, and work hard alongside your children. Zones can do more for your children's character training than almost anything else.

I share this explanation about sweat equity in the chapter about my sixth daughter because it was right around the time of her birth, and surely over the decade since, that we have developed the idea of sweat equity into a foundational part of our family's culture. By the time Trinity was born, there was no way a momma with six little daughters, all under eight years old, could manage every affair of the home singlehandedly.

Although my system began on a shaky foundation, with children not much accustomed to hard work, after several revisions of our plan, we landed on one that works relatively well. When Trinity was a baby, I began by dividing the house into sections and passing my three oldest children different areas of the house to be in charge of. Over the years since, many of the children have had different jobs that involved varying levels of responsibility according to their age and capability.

When Trinity was two, she began "helping" by spraying water in a spritzer bottle on windows to keep her busy while we worked. By the time she was three, she moved up to "chief baseboard cleaner," where on cleaning day she would be given a damp rag to wash the baseboards. Somewhere around four, she moved up to wall scrubber, door jamb cleaner, and bathroom trash emptier. At five, she could make her bed every morning and be responsible for her basic grooming...although at times her hairdo choices were questionable. As she continued to grow, we gave her "zones" that grew in terms of size and responsibility until now, at age ten, she is responsible for all of our laundry.

I have children who work and contribute to our household. Some zones require the consistent maintenance of only one child, like our shoe closet maintained by six-year-old Ransom. Some zones, like the kitchen, have a team because of the sheer scope and size of meal planning, shopping, cooking, cleaning, pantry and refrigerator maintenance for a family of seventeen! But, the overall goal is to have a child who is responsible not just for their own needs, but responsive to the needs of others.

Laundry duty has taught Trinity quite a bit. She keeps a list for our grocery shoppers for when she needs detergent, bleach, stain-remover, and dryer sheets. She has to be aware what days her brothers need their football uniforms, make sure there are clean towels for swim practice, and enough towels in the bathrooms to dry all seventeen of us. Trinity needs to know what special outfits we need ready for an event and have them prepared ahead of time...because as everyone knows, the quickest way to blow mom's top is to be missing a shirt or a certain skirt for one kid out of fifteen when we are already running late. Trinity loves to help me pick out an outfit for my special dates with David and takes incredible pride in a nicely pressed pair of white linen pants for mama. And while many parents may think I do this out of convenience for me, let me please assure you that there is far more than just my convenience at stake. For the record, teaching a child to do the laundry is not convenient at first. It can involve several costly lessons up front, like the time my brand new white denim jacket was washed and dried with a pair of shorts containing a pocket full of glitter crayons!

You see, Trinity is not our little laundry slave. She is an avid participant in what makes the wheels of this gigantic family go round. While she is busy on laundry duty, with all it entails, she knows that Kemper and Glory are preparing her meals and making her favorite dinner. She is aware that Judson cleans her bathroom. Ransom keeps track of her shoes. Bliss is in charge of our "library" and all the school supplies, including Trinity's. Every child in this family has a zone or part of the household responsibility, and therefore, everyone is serving one another. We are working together, pouring in sweat equity.

Sweat equity is a heck of a lot more than just a better way to divide up household chores. I'll warn you that when you begin to implement this type of structure, you're in for a rude awakening... at least I was.

You see, the first thing you need to know about implementing a zone infrastructure into your household management is that initially, the job is way less about getting the work done and far more about putting the character training into the heart of your child. Zones take time to develop and below I have listed several ways our family institutes a zone system:

1. Don't change zones often. In my household, the children are likely to be on a specific zone for a one-year minimum.
2. Zones work best when an area is well defined, as in, from this doorway on, any-

thing and everything in the bathroom, or everything to do with the garage.

3. Be prepared to teach. Over and over again.

4. You can't point and tell. You have to squat alongside your child and do it with them. Repeatedly. On your hands and knees. This method of management is not for the weak or timid.

5. Zones are initially less about the work getting done and more about training work ethic, excellence, and efficiency into your child. Expect the training time to take longer and be more difficult than you had previously thought possible.

6. Zones are given in terms of age, capability, and responsibility. I may take suggestions for zones or consider changing them every now and then, but it's not like everyone gets to choose their own zones and I do everything left over. If I took requests, it wouldn't really be cultivating the heart of a servant, that would be a democracy...which this household is definitely not. Our home is under a benevolent dictatorship. When I am called Napoleon, I console myself with the thought that the reference is strictly because of my height. But you can be sure

I'll never be confused with Mother Teresa.

7. Zones not only teach work ethic, train efficiency, and keep your house running smoother without one parent in charge of every minute detail, but they build family loyalty, buy-in, and create an inner strength in your child that is far more implicating than simply getting a chore done.

8. Most surprisingly, I don't pay for zones. If the children want to make money, they have to come up with a job outside the scope of their normal work, negotiate for a price, and complete the job to my specifications and on time.

Growing up this way, I see Trinity as one of the hardest working, mentally mature and responsible children we have raised. We often joke that we could just have the "Talk to Trin" show because she is so adept at boiling issues down to simple and insightful truths. Her schoolwork needs little to no prodding from me, because her time is precious and valuable with all she is responsible for in the laundry arena.

Are there days we still struggle? Yes, absolutely.

Is the laundry all folded according to my father's Marine Corps exacting standards? Not every time. Maybe not even most of the time. As parents, expect excellence, but know it's a process. Interject lots of humor, love, and encouragement, but don't shrink back from the inevitable confrontations. We'll eventually see the fruit of all that sweat equity mature into a well-developed, well-rounded, hard-working young adult.

Sweat Equity or Child Labor?

Recently we had a family of guests staying over. After dinner, as my children went to work clearing the table, cleaning the kitchen, and vacuuming the floors, the ten-year-old guest asked me how much my kids get paid for doing these "chores."

He was dumbfounded when I replied, "They don't."

"Well, 'cause at my house I get paid for every chore I do like that. If I do somethin' like that, I get a dollar." And funny, this child enjoyed a meal at my home, but he never said thank you. He watched my children get right to work, but felt no desire to help or serve in any way because there was nothing in it for him.

Folks, you don't have to agree with me, but I believe allowances are wrong. Paying a kid for simply being a member of the family is crazy. Paying them for helping out around the house, for simple things like cleaning up after a meal, making their bed, and keeping their room clean is not beneficial in the long run. These are bare minimum manners and the basest of expectations. I have plenty of kiddos and there is more than enough work to go around: laundry, dishes, meal planning, bathrooms, trash duty...oh my, the list is literally a mile long. But my children don't get paid for any of it. Our kids are building sweat equity into our family...learning to love those they live life with by serving them consistently.

When I say a child should work for the family, most parents look at me like I have suggested slave labor. But you know what? Children are happier for the work and responsibility! There is no "what's in it for me if I help you clean out this fridge?" mentality. Instead, they are joyful about their work knowing that other family members are working just as hard for them! While Trinity is over the laundry job, she'll never complain about the cooking that Kemper and Glory are doing—she is too busy working and so are they! Courson doesn't have time to balk at the condition of the bathroom (Judson's job) because he is too busy getting the closet back in order every morning. When Trinity falls behind, everyone jumps in to help, because they all understand what it's like to lose your footing in your zone. They would never expect her to pay them for it.

So how do my children earn money? How do they learn the value of a dollar and to budget? Anything out of the ordinary scope of day-to-day work is up for discussion and negotiation. Recently, the boys have been working hard to get a set of Beyblades. They've been coming up with all kinds of jobs...cleaning out the van, washing all the vehicles' exteriors, weeding, cleaning up the side yard from dog messes, and trimming some of the smaller hedges. The price I pay varies on length of job, diligence in their effort, and attitude. They work hard for every penny. They are learning that money is not so easy to make, and so it shouldn't be blown haphazardly.

They also learn the value of a dollar by watching daddy work hard, and mom deliberate over purchases. The kids have learned how to bargain hunt and negotiate by tagging along with mom at yard sales and even when I am at a retail store. As they get older, we devise scenarios where they are given a budget to do a project and must negotiate their way into completing it on time and for the right price. These are all practical skills that come in handy in real life, where there ain't nobody paying you...for just bein' you.

So if you choose to give allowances, look carefully into the attitude and heart of your child's work ethic. Do they work willingly, with a joyful heart? Or are they constantly asking "How much will you pay me if I do this for you?"

My wholehearted conviction is that pouring sweat equity into our family builds love, trust, and loyalty like no other decision we make as parents.

Cleaning Day Isn't About a Clean House

We have cleaning day once a week. A person may think we do this to actually get the house clean. But they would be wrong. Having a clean house is likely third or fourth on the list of why we have cleaning day.

The priority is character training.

When I began this weekly foray into insanity, I had six children and Daly Kay was nine. At that time I only had three kids who could really do much to help. Glory Grace and Kemper (at three and two years old) mostly followed behind us and destroyed any work we actually got done. It was frustrating...for several years.

After much perseverance, the kids finally got

the hint that I was going to call them back to the job every time it was not done properly.

Those were the *easy* days. Now, we have thirteen children working to clean a house that should only take three hard workers an hour and a half to get done. So the challenge becomes not just getting the house clean but making sure everyone is actually working.

You see, I have noticed there may be kids who are very busy, but they really aren't getting much done. For those children, I have to teach them to focus on the job at hand, and in most cases, stay pretty close to their side during cleaning day. If I don't, they wander off and get lost in the general shuffle. Last week, I caught one of my younger daughters bolting off into the living room. I got onto her to get back to her job! "Right! More talk, more panic!" she answered in her flibbity-gibbit way and *BIY-YONG* she went back to the sunroom where the Mount Everest of laundry was being climbed by four brave souls.

But that's the way a lot of kids approach work. "If I look busy, I'll get by with it." And worst of all is when the child is actually looking busy by bossing everyone else around and delegating work, while they have no sweat on their own brow. Aw, man...*those* kids make me angry on a whole 'nother level.

Moms and dads, diligence is sincerely one of the most important character traits you can train your child in. Seriously evaluate your child... today...this week...and make sure they are learning to work hard. Make sure they do their work well, and train them to go above and beyond.

Simple things like leaving a dish to "soak" in the sink. Just scrub the bleeping thing and finish the job.

Leaving an empty roll on the toilet paper hanger. Really?

Walking by a stray pencil or sock on the floor.

Leaving the piece of trash next to the trashcan. Or worse, walking past a full trashcan and not taking it out—or taking it out but not replacing the bag!

When a job needs to be done, take the time to stop working yourself, and seriously evaluate the level of effort and accomplishment each child is making. If there is a slacker, GET ON IT.

We all know adults who are great at looking busy, but they never actually do a darn thing. We can look at the fruit of their lives and see that we do not want that for our children. If your child won't apply themselves in the small mundane work of cleaning the house or working in the yard, they will likely never strive for greatness in their education or employment.

Diligence is not something they will learn by simply watching us work hard. It is something they must be trained in. Constantly. For years. Diligence is definitely not the easiest thing to teach our children, but arguably the most important.

If our children possess diligence, they will overcome anything thrown at them.

Doers vs. Delegators

Last year, we said goodbye to a good friend who has managed our favorite restaurant for several years. Lloyd had been a big help to our not-so-easy-to-accommodate family. Always smiling, he has been the example to my kids of servant-hearted diligence more times than I can count. Lloyd left our area for a better opportunity in the Northeast, and this served my children as an example of the rewards we can reap when we employ these valuable virtues in our lives.

When people ask me emphatically, "How do you do it?" I smile and say that I am in *upper management* now." But that wasn't always so. When I had five children and my oldest was seven, I was the swab of every deck. I did it all. Sure the kids "helped," but their helping looked a lot more like messing up most of my work while I tried to remain calm and keep them ~~distracted~~ working.

All that turned into training. Then as they learned, they took over certain aspects of the household jobs. Eventually, they became masters of their "zones." Laundry, kitchen, bathrooms, pantry/fridges, my bedroom, living areas, school room...all became privatized areas of responsibility for individuals to organize and keep clean. I had moved into management. A promotion indeed!

I began to notice something though. As my team had watched me sweat and work with them, alongside them on my knees scrubbing...they took pride in relieving me from my duties. So much so that I rarely had to delegate anymore. It became a race to them to say, "Let me do that for you, Mommy!" And here is where my last teaching point begins...

Moms and dads...pay attention. Have you witnessed a child that when asked to do something, they quickly delegate that job to someone else? Oh, the job gets done...but not by them? Tune in, folks. This is a kid who has watched those in authority pass off work instead of sweat, and WORSE, considers themselves on par with their authority instead of a willing, loving, serving, contributing family member.

This is dangerous.

First of all, it will tick off every sibling and build resentment toward that child.

Second, the self-appointed delegator becomes very "wise in their own eyes" and rarely serves anyone but themselves.

And last but certainly not least, that child will grow into a lazy adult who will be looked down upon by everyone but themselves. BIG no-no.

I never saw Lloyd pass off any type of work. I saw him do everything from moving cars through for valets, moving tables, clearing place settings, even running to get water for me when I had a coughing fit in the middle of a meal. His team rallied around him and worked better with him because they knew he would stay late, work hard, and do whatever it took to make an event run smoothly. With a manager willing to do anything, the team was willing to do anything.

Moms and dads, there is no short-cut to raising a hard worker. Our kids have to watch us sweat and work along-side of them for years before they take it on as a character trait for themselves. We simply cannot delegate them into working hard, telling them what to do at every turn, and micro-managing them to death.

So if you listen around your home today and hear "the self-appointed delegator" telling everyone else what to do, or worse, giving out orders to others that you just gave to that very delegator... make some serious changes. In yourself, and in the life of that child.

Because trust me, they won't start out in life in "upper management."

The Pay-Off

I witnessed the pay-off big time last year right before Christmas. We moved into a new home. It was a crazy whirlwind week and I was amazed at the endless amounts of hard work our kids poured into moving this three-ring circus. It showed me that all those lessons on hard work and diligence, as well as teaching them to pour themselves into their family, had dividends beyond what I could have ever imagined.

My kids worked their fannies off. Several all-nighters in a row of packing, lifting, loading, moving, cleaning. Never a complaint, rarely an argument.

Ryli watched wee ones and kept them amazingly occupied amidst an explosion of boxes and clothing. When the kids were napping, she was packing or clearing out junk. I would leave Glory in a room with boxes and she'd just pack away for hours, leaving only for a slice of pizza. Daly Kay was not only a great worker bee, but she was phenomenal at reading the pulse of the group...bringing Coke and coffee to tired souls and encouraging us when we were all about to bite each others' heads off. Bliss literally worked nonstop. Kemper was constantly packing and moving boxes. Trinity was a great helper with the little ones. And probably most impressive (for his age) was Courson. That little man worked incessantly, every bit as hard as any grown up. Every night at midnight, I was telling him to go to bed and he was just begging to keep working.

Kids can do amazing things. They can be as diligent as any adult. Somehow, many parents think kids deserve a soft ride. Lots of adults I know think that if they ask their children to work hard, they are somehow robbing them of this carefree childhood that we have been hoodwinked into thinking our children are owed.

The Bible tells us that diligence is a man's precious possession (Proverbs 12:27 NASB), and the hand of the diligent makes rich (Proverbs 10:4 ESV). You can be dumb and diligent and still make it pretty darn far in this world, but smart and lazy will leave you poor and lonely.

Make every effort to train your children to be hard workers. Raise the bar by encouraging them to do all their work to their utmost ability. Give them opportunities to serve others without expecting anything in return, and seriously reconsider if you are giving your kids an allowance. People love what they invest in, but not always what they are paid for. By investing "sweat equity" into the family with hard work, they are investing a harvest into your family. And when it comes time for you to reap that harvest, you'll be glad for all those years of challenging sowing.

7.

Never Leave a Man Behind

*Be strong and of good courage; do not be
afraid, nor be dismayed, for the Lord your God is
with you wherever you go.*

Joshua 1:9 NKJV

David and I had six little girls, ten years old and
under. We began to explore the idea of adoption a
little more seriously after several of our friends at
church had either adopted from a foreign country
or had gone through a foster-to-adopt initiative.
When Trinity was just a couple of months old, we
began the state of Florida's home-study classes.
These classes were designed to educate potential
foster and adoptive parents of the inherent per-
ils and challenges families face as they integrate
children with an abusive past into their families.

Of the ten couples, David and I were the only ones who had biological children, and bringing Trinity every week was a necessity since I was nursing her. The hypotheticals posed in class and the seemingly hopeless diagnoses these potential parents were given struck me as harsh. More times than not I found my experiences in raising children left me at odds with the curriculum's assessments. My husband and I filled out the mountains of paperwork and went through all the screening and fingerprinting.

We prepared our house for our impending home-study assessment. Finally the big day arrived and our social worker came late in the evening to meet our family. After we had put the girls to bed, we continued with her interview and evaluation. She finally looked at both of us and said, "Mr. and Mrs. Reback, you have a lovely home. But I am sorry to say that you are just not going to be placed with children from the state. You know, kids adopted from the state don't come saying *yes ma'am and no ma'am* like yours do."

Wow. Thanks for that, Miss Single-and-26-Year-Old-Social-Worker.

I quickly reminded her that my children didn't "come" saying yes ma'am and no ma'am either. They were TAUGHT. My blood was beginning to boil as I felt anger welling up inside of me. We had been trucking an hour south back and forth for one night every week for ten weeks, paying a babysitter for five children, and answering hundreds of personal questions. The thought that the state found us "unfit" to accept a sibling group when we were the only experienced parents in the class had my gasket about to blow. But her mind was made up and her assessment complete.

I'll never forget what happened next...

My husband looked right into her spectacled eyes and said, "That's all right. We are going to get a baby anyhow."

With that, Miss Social Worker closed her folder, bid us a good evening, and walked out our front door leaving all my dreams of adoption crumbling behind her.

Angry as a wet cat, I looked at David through narrowed eyes. "Why on earth would you ever say that to her? Now she'll never give us any children! She thinks we only want BABIES! We said we wanted a sibling group! Whatever possessed you to say something so crazy? Adopting babies is for people who can't HAVE babies! We CAN! Why would we ever do that???"

Calmly he just looked into my eyes and held my hand.

"I've known for a long time. You'll see. We are going to get a baby."

Two weeks later, David and I were at a group track workout with the children. I was running along and a mom who was also looking to adopt shared an interesting story with me about a baby born prematurely. An attorney had called her and her husband to see if they would think about adopting the child. She had recently discovered she was pregnant and they decided this adoption was not for them...but maybe David and I would consider the scenario? On the way home I brought it up to David. He told me to call the attorney the next day.

The following afternoon while the girls were at swim practice, I called the attorney. He was a business litigator who had stumbled into adoption through various scenarios at his church, and this case was no exception. He explained that the baby had been born extremely premature, had been in the hospital for two weeks, was weighing less than two pounds, and the bill was probably going to be in excess of a *million dollars.*

"When can we see the baby?"

I was quaking at the thought of every challenge he had just listed, but I knew David would at least want the opportunity to see the child.

"This is where everyone hangs up. Did you hear all that I just told you? The bill is going to be more than a million dollars!"

I told him I was not hard of hearing but we at least wanted the opportunity to meet him.

"I'll meet you at the hospital at 8:30 tonight," he said.

I could almost hear him shaking his head.

David and I arrived at the hospital a little earlier than 8:30. Unexpectedly, I saw an old acquaintance who was there with her baby in the NICU step-down unit. Apparently her baby had also been born quite early, but now that he was just over four pounds, he was almost ready to go home. She invited me in to hold him and I marveled at his size. Four pounds was small! I couldn't even imagine what a baby half that size was going to look like.

I didn't have to wonder long. A gruffly handsome older gentleman walked by wearing the standard attorney uniform: starched shirt, monogrammed cuff, perfectly pressed pants, and shiny shoes. His large frame was crowned with a thinned and graying head of hair. His squared out shoulders bent over the NICU sink as he scrubbed his hands vigorously.

David and I introduced ourselves and he

scoped us out. As if his large, booming voice and solid frame weren't intimidating enough, he had a black eye and a fairly good scrape across his nose. "Don't mind the bandage...I got my clock cleaned in cage fighting this week."

Oh, great. An attorney that's also a trained killer.

Just what I expected.

Nothing could have prepared me for what lay in that isolette.

Tiny...barely bigger than my hand, and covered in a small cap of brown hair lay a little *boy*. His thin skin revealed nearly every vein and capillary, his red feet uncovered and miniscule. His narrowly opened eyes staring off into the distance. I just stood there astounded.

By the end of our time together the attorney had grilled us in an interview and decided that since he had been given the status of legal guardian over the baby, he would clear us through the hospital to come visit any time. We agreed to come and speak with the hospital administration the next day about the billing process and we could take it from there.

David and I rode home in stunned silence.

The following day we took all the girls to the hospital as David and the attorney wrangled through all the possible payment scenarios for this now "abandoned" child with the hospital's administration. After a few hours it was decided that the child was "indigent," and therefore, neither the attorney nor the prospective adoptive parents should be held liable for his incurring bills. In fact, the hospital would file for Medicaid on his behalf and this wee miracle's bill would be ZERO.

Nada.

Zip.

As in *free.*

Within twenty-four hours God had given us the potential to adopt a son and also removed his **$1,000,000+** bill. With that in mind we went to visit him as we left the administrative wing of the hospital and the girls were full of questions. David kept them occupied in the hallway as the attorney and I walked into the NICU.

Scrubbed up and walking toward his isolette, a nurse that knew our family from church saw us with the attorney. She stood there in disbelief and dropped her files of paperwork and charts.

"NO WAY! JUST NO WAY! I have been praying for this little boy to get a family and in YOU walk?? Oh my gosh, no way!!!" Her approval resounded and loud cheers of joy and excitement brought more than just a little bit of attention as I neared the baby's bed. Beeping alarms monitored his vitals, tubes out of his nose and wires taped to his chest, he looked more like a caterpillar than a baby. I ignored everyone's questions and just wondered over and over in my head if this was indeed *my* son. The attorney placed his "NICU parent" bracelet on my wrist and left me alone for a few minutes. Well...as alone as I *could* be with a bevy of nurses prematurely congratulating me and asking me questions while simultaneously warning me and clucking their doubt.

Later that night David and I returned alone to the NICU and spoke with doctors and nurses who had been over the baby's care since he was born. Giving us their best and worst case scenarios, they tried to prepare us to make our most informed decision.

What kind of challenges might this boy face?

Blindness...as he was born before his corneas had been fully developed and it was not known what quality of sight, if any, he would have.

Disabilities...he had a brain bleed early on that had mostly resolved itself but the long term effects were unknown.

Down Syndrome...he had several physical markers but as of yet they had not done chromosomal testing.

His head was horribly misshapen because the nurses were all right-handed. They had laid him on his left side continually to make changing his diaper and electronic leads easier. And then there was the constant threat of NEC, a condition that kills many preemies. NEC stands for Necrotizing Enterocolitis, where the premature baby's intestinal lining becomes infected and begins to die. Since their intestinal tract is not designed to be taking food this early, many babies succumb to the infection and, even with incredible medical intervention, still die. This baby boy was on formula, an even tougher substance on their stomachs and intestines. A thought occurred to me as the nurse practitioner explained the risks of formula and preemies. I was still breastfeeding Trinity who was nine months old at the time. Would I be able to pump and give this boy a better chance at life?

Now the NICU staff was incredulous. When the attorney heard, he just couldn't believe it either. This little baby could be breastfed and his multiple risk factors reduced if I could give him mother's milk? Again David and I drove home very late that night in stunned silence.

Once in bed, I tossed and turned endlessly. Sleep

was evading my every request. Praying, worrying, thinking, whimpering, I just keep flopping around in bed. Well past midnight I sat bolt upright in bed and almost yelled, "WE LEFT A MAN BEHIND! WE NEVER LEAVE A MAN BEHIND!"

You see, after Ryli's many hospital jaunts, we had decided on a family policy. David and I vowed to never leave a man behind. Even though to date, our policy only involved our six daughters, we promised one another that if ever a child was in a hospital *one* or *both* of us would be there continuously. This policy had evolved into never leaving a young child at sports practice, alone at a party, or alone *anywhere*. It required a whole 'nuther level of commitment from us as parents and it had forced us to carefully evaluate all of our activities by whether we could truthfully commit to staying with the child at all times. And now here it was, way into the wee hours of the morning, and I was convinced that we had left one of *our own* behind...alone in a hospital...without our protection or love.

And we knew. *He was our son.*

I dressed myself quickly and drove directly to the hospital.

Somewhere around 3:00 a.m. on August 12th, I became the proud mother of six daughters *and a son.*

The next eight weeks were fraught with challenges, and our little boy was finally given a name, Jon Courson. He defied all of the earlier assessments about his health, diagnostics, and disabilities and grew to be a strappingly strong, albeit still small, young man. While I sat most days and nights in the hospital, David busied himself with the girls by building "Fort Courson"—a tree house that eventually involved roofing, electricity, windows, and an air conditioning unit. It was a crazy, glorious, faith-building, miracle-after-miracle period in our lives.

And I have to admit, the best phone call I ever made was to Miss 26-Year-Old-Social-Worker who had originally denied our adoption. The incredulity in her voice when I asked for our home-study was priceless. "We got a baby!" I told her, with a less than perfect Christian attitude. I never again doubted my husband's intuition.

Today's parents are given so many options for education and activity. The propensity to fill our children's days in the name of all the extra-curricular activities and tutoring, with every intention to give our children the best and most competitive edge in life, can often leave us with very little actual time spent together. Our "Never Leave a Man Behind" policy originated with stays in various hospitals, but eventually extended into all areas of our children's lives. As a child, I had endured several adverse situations. These influenced my decision to always be present throughout my children's adolescence in the hopes of avoiding such scenarios on their behalf. It hasn't always been easy, by any stretch of the imagination, but it has always been worth it.

This policy has not included conflict-avoidance or even spurred the idea that mom and dad will always be there to solve every issue or event of injustice. We don't hover, but merely stay present at a distance and available. In most cases where conflict arises, we can give honest feedback to our child regarding who was really at fault and afterwards teach or train them how to better handle such situations. The policy was not meant to be something that we tied ourselves to, but in most cases we found that it necessitated the serious evaluation of every event or activity we committed to. It also set precedents for things like dinner time...we would "Never Leave a Man Behind" to eat alone. Dinner was kept a family event and at least four nights out of seven, even David was present. When swim team schedules became such that our biggest kids didn't get home until 8 p.m.

and we had six small children waiting to eat dinner with them, we had to find another way to keep the practice going by changing when and where.

This policy also made us consider the value of fleeting Saturdays. Did we honestly WANT to spend every Saturday torn apart as a family going birthday party to birthday party, swim meet to swim meet? No.

Again, we reviewed our priorities and scaled back to events we were all invited to. For us, that made it easy...who wants to add in an extra twelve to fifteen people? We chose competitions that were actually valuable and with enough time between races for them to see marked improvement.

The "Never Leave a Man Behind" policy is not meant as a law of contention, but actually, it helps prioritize and protect, not just your children, but also your time. There are a great many things we say "no" to as a family, but the things we chose to say YES to are actually the priorities we truly enjoy and it's time well spent together.

Eventually, this policy shaped our family's culture to usually include our children in things that previously only adults would attend. Political forums? Kids would come with us. Fundraisers? Why not include the children? Client dinners? At least the oldest children could come...they became a great window into my husband's character and work ethic.

Soon we noticed in our social circle that parents and even grandparents were including more of their family in their previously adult-only events...and that made us glad. Children, as "adults in the making," need to feel *valued* and *wanted* in our "big person" society. The school model of constant age segregation has done more harm than good in relaying the wisdom of those more advanced in years and experience. It is one of my greatest desires to see this country again value one another as people...not old people, young people, middle-aged people...but just people. Including our children in nearly every area of our lives—committing to BE TOGETHER—has shown those around us that children have valuable opinions, can form incredible conclusions, and should be given worth and place in society.

I invite you to consider how you may want to incorporate a policy such as "Never Leave a Man Behind." Give it a try for three months and see how the relationship dynamics, priorities, and values of your family change.

Of course there comes a time when we must incorporate more and more independence into the lives of our children as they grow and demon-strate responsibility. But in my experience, early on, families tend to spend too little time together, which can cause children to have a false sense of wisdom and independence way ahead of their own understanding of what repercussions their actions may have.

8.

Liberty Brings Freedom

Now the Lord is the Spirit; and where the Spirit of the Lord is, there is liberty.

2 Corinthians 3:17 NKJV

Our second adoption came thirteen months after Courson was added to our family. This addition marked a turning point in our lives that I'm not so sure we realized at the time, but we came to revel in the results. We had a name picked out long before we met her...Liberty Cross. She would have my initials. We anticipated her arrival privately as friends and family already thought we were a little on the crazy side for having so many children.

I first laid eyes on my new daughter when she was just a few minutes old. A nurse brought her into a private room in the hospital where David and I gazed lovingly at her beauty. Ruddy complexion, curly black hair, brown eyes like mine... we were in love.

In the adoption process, you never really know what to expect. David and I have learned through our adoption stories that, while the walk itself may not always be pretty, the journey is well worth the trip and the tribulations. By the time a woman has come to the conclusion that her baby is better off without her, the level of problematic relationships and family drama can be unprecedented. Often times we are faced with the heartbreak of the ensuing loss the birth mother faces and the simultaneous joy we receive with each miraculous new addition to our family.

Liberty's adoption was full of such challenges and surprises.

Not the least of which came a few days after her birth. She came home at forty-eight hours old and within another twenty-four, she was covered in small red bumps. Her entire complexion was already dark and mottled so we took her to our pediatrician. The doctor began to ask us some questions about Liberty's birth parents, about whom we had very few answers to give. For various reasons, our attorney had found it difficult to place this child with any other family that had expressed interest in adoption. David and I didn't really ask much when given the opportunity to add to our family. The pediatrician then pointed out that Liberty had "Mongolian spots" above her buttocks as well as several other indicators that led her to believe that Liberty was biracial.

Surprise, surprise!

And while it was a surprise to me, David admitted he'd had an inkling all along. We had been given the opportunity to adopt Liberty fairly early on in the pregnancy, and David said he just had a feeling this child of ours would be biracial.

Interestingly enough, as I was growing up in my small Texas town, I was often teased because of my mother's dark skin that she was black. This was 1970s folks. *In the South.* People didn't mix. "Birds of a feather flock together" was taught as some sort of twisted biblical saying, and I never saw a biracial couple until I was grown. My mother's dark skin from her French Canadian heritage would sure come in helpful to my newest and most adorable daughter. She would have someone in her family that would look just like her!

Our church had plenty of families that looked like a mini representation of the United Nations due to foreign and local interracial adoptions, so Liberty never felt out of place. I'll admit her skin and hair textures gave this ol' white girl more than a few challenges and I found myself asking every African American lady in Target what to do about them.

My favorite story about Liberty as a baby and dealing with people who saw our family as an anomaly came when she was about two years old. At the time I had a stroller with six seats in it, and I had taken the children to a large local political gathering. David was following behind, a few minutes late from work, so just the twelve children (at the time) and I stood in a crowd. Daly Kay was fourteen.

A woman walked up and began throwing probing questions at me with a rude and incredulous tone of voice. Normally, I can answer questions curtly, and by cutting off eye contact, most people get the hint to move on. Not this lady. She apparently felt entitled to know everything about us, including if all the children were mine and which of them were adopted.

Now had she asked the question *politely*... as in..."Have you adopted any of these beautiful babies?" I may have answered her "yes." But when she asked the question pointing directly at Liberty, my mean mama bear side came out and I declared I had not adopted any of them. Daly Kay looked at me and a smile began to form in the corners of her mouth.

"NONE of them are adopted??" She was now speaking louder and ruder, if that was even possible.

"Nope. Not one. They are all mine."

"Even that one?" she asked, pointing rudely into Liberty's face.

"Yes, even that one. She's my LOVE CHILD." Daly Kay burst into laughter and the woman *harummffffed* and walked away disgusted, just in time for David to come cruising up the sidewalk to meet us.

"DAAAADDDDYYYYY!" every little child squealed with delight, and I ran to hug my man. Love child indeed. Her father and I loved each other very much, and we were blessed to be given this gift from our Heavenly Father whose love and providence had brought this miracle into our lives. Who cared what color she was????

So the turning point we crossed by bringing Liberty into our family was more than just breaking through some racial barrier. We had now crossed into the "we don't give a flip anymore about what others think" territory and the freedom (get it, *Liberty?*) that brought into our lives was incredible. It oozed into just about every facet of our being.

Parenting is a tough gig. You're going to make different decisions than your friends make. You're going to parent differently than your folks did. You're going to disagree with a schoolteacher or some sort of authority in a field, and you're going to have to grow a thick skin about it. You have to follow your calling, your ministry, your purpose as an individual and as a family...and you're going to have to give yourself the LIBERTY from what others think about your decisions. When you get there, and you *will*, the freedom you experience will have been worth the struggle.

Defending One Another

Growing up can be hard. Every kid is going to get picked on from time to time. Wise is the parent who seeks to teach through the difficulty rather than remove the child from such an incredible opportunity to learn. One such challenge occurred recently for our young Liberty.

At eight years old, she is a striking tower of beauty. My pediatrician jokes that since I am five foot one, I am going to have a tough time explaining how I have a daughter playing in the WNBA. She's tall, she's pretty, and she's an absolute jumping bean of energy. Several Sundays ago, she was happily playing in her classroom at church when a young boy began to make fun of her because of her short hair. He mocked her saying she was a boy, and to top it off, she was *ugly*, too. Apparently this travesty continued on for quite some time and Liberty was deeply hurt. She came home and shared with her sisters later at bedtime about this kid's rudeness. When I found out the following day, I was *livid*.

I called every kid to the dining room table. I asked Liberty to stand up and share with all of us exactly what had happened in Sunday school. With a quaking voice, she gave us the heart-wrenching details about the exchange and every sibling waivered between hot anger and heartbreak.

I asked Liberty to come to me. I cupped her adorable face in my hands and told her she was the most breathtakingly beautiful little princess I had ever seen. Her lips quivered, but her eyes sparkled, mixed with joy and tears. I told her that little twerp was probably picking on her because he liked her, but never-she-mind because he was obviously a jerk and had no chance with such a princess! Then, I began to teach...

I taught Liberty WHAT TO DO when ugliness like that rears its head in a classroom, a playground, or any place she may find herself intimidated. I asked her to pretend that I was the scoundrel making fun of her. I told her to answer me back, looking me dead in the eyes and using a tone of voice that says, "Don't mess with me boy." For ten minutes straight, with every sibling looking on, I implored her to answer my rude comments LOUDER, and to look intently into my eyes. I showed her how to position her body to say "I mean it" and how to firmly walk away from the confrontation in such a manner that twerpo moves on. Within minutes, her confidence soared and we could see that she now knew how to handle such adversity.

But my teaching had barely begun.

Next, I turned my attention to her four brothers, who were also in that same Sunday school room when Liberty was being mocked.

"Where were you boys? What were you doing when Liberty was being made fun of by this kid?" It was a small class and truly there was no way an exchange like this could have happened where not one of her brothers was privy to the challenge.

One brother looked at another. Their eyes darted back and forth. They looked at Liberty, and I could see the boys understood immediately what I was getting at.

"Look men, you've got an obligation to keep an eye out for each other and for your sisters. When one of you gets bombarded or bullied, each of you should come to the rescue. Liberty has to learn how to handle this on her own, but the truth is that with four brothers around her, she should never be left alone!"

Then I began to role-play with the brothers what it looked like to stand up for one another and to stand up for their sister. They apologized to Liberty and she was more than happy to forgive. But an important lesson was forged for sure.

Role-Playing and Dealing with Adversity

Moms and dads, one of the most valuable tools you can use in training your children is role-playing. Role-playing gives children the ability to practice a situation in advance of a public trial. Role-playing how to handle a difficult conversation with a friend or an authority figure, role-playing how to deal with bullies, or role-playing how to show proper emotions or apologies that are difficult can minimize nerves and truly prepare a child for adverse situations like very few other methods actually can. When we give our children the benefit of practicing eye contact, posture, and tone of voice ahead of time, they can maneuver through such issues, prepared with strength and confidence. Role-playing can be a lifesaver when teaching your children how to deal with stranger danger, child predators, or even preparing them to be home alone. Fire drills, emergency-type situation practice, and even how to dial 911 are all important uses for role-playing.

Although I've shared my little challenge with Liberty to demonstrate role-playing, my all-time favorite story using this method of preparation comes from David's childhood.

Permission to Fight or Flub It Up

When David was in middle school, he kept getting roughed up by a bunch of boys who would routinely intimidate him into giving them his lunch money. After several weeks of going hungry, David decided he had had enough. He came home and told his dad about these ruffians and said that if he fought them, David would likely be the one pegged for starting a fight and he was going to wind up in the principal's office. In what I think is the most profound and wisest thing David's father ever said, he replied to his pre-pubescent son that indeed, Paul, David's father, *wanted* that phone call from the principal. "You go ahead and do what you have to do. I'll gladly come pick you up from school."

Paul then proceeded to teach David a rudimentary understanding of boxing and sent his son off to school the next day hoping for change.

David didn't disappoint. The lunch money bullies tried to extort his $5 and reluctantly, David landed the first punch. While it wasn't exactly a fair fight with five against one, David managed to land a few good licks before being sent to the principal's office for the ensuing punishment. True to his word, his dad picked up David and *congratulated* him on becoming a man who would defend himself no matter the odds. I'm not sure the situation would have ended so well if David's dad hadn't:

1. Given his son permission to fight. David thought he was doing the right thing by turning the other cheek, but his hungry belly and his frustrated conscience told him there had to be a better way.
2. Given his son some role-playing and some fundamental fighting skills. We live in a fallen world, folks. Our kids are going to

face adversity to which sometimes there is no better answer than to defend themselves or their defenseless peers. Teach your kids how to stick up for themselves, their siblings, and those in need of a friend.

3. Given his son the freedom to get into trouble (for the right reasons) or the freedom to fail. Sometimes the school rules don't allow for justice to prevail. Sometimes a child may take justice into their own hands and do so wrongly. Kids will make mistakes along the way as they navigate through childhood and adolescence, and we have to give them that freedom as parents. It's not always neat and pretty, folks, but it is *beautiful*...especially when they make the *right* wrong decision!

So learn a lesson from my little Liberty Belle (a nickname we gave her when she chipped her front tooth just like the bell in Philadelphia and added the extra "e" for beauty). Give yourself the freedom to parent differently. Give yourself and your children the freedom to break the rules for the right reasons, defend the defenseless, and the freedom to fail.

It's liberating...in more ways than you can imagine.

9.

Fearfully and Wonderfully Made

I will praise You, for I am fearfully and wonderfully made; Marvelous are Your works, And that my soul knows very well.

Psalm 139:14 NKJV

David and I had the opportunity to take the children on the vacation of a lifetime. We had traveled the Mediterranean by cruise ship, stayed in Cairo visiting the Pyramids for a week, and we were finishing the trip in Israel. The morning after we arrived, I realized I had been feeling a little nauseous. Curious as to whether this upset stomach was the result of drinking the local water or something *else*, I took a pregnancy test.

Doesn't everyone travel with a pregnancy test?

The double pink lines quickly revealed that we

would be having another baby! I excitedly jumped back into bed and told David. He responded with joy, but throughout the day, his facial expressions didn't match his words. I blew it off and decided he must be tired.

We got home a couple of weeks later and I went to my obstetrician's office. Everything seemed to be going along quite smoothly as my pregnancy progressed. It was a crazy busy time in our lives... we were building a new home for which David was the general contractor. I was homeschooling. We had four children on swim team with practices every day. Trinity, Courson, and Liberty were all under three years old. Weeks flew by and it seemed that when my prenatal appointments came up, David was always too busy. He would call ten minutes before my appointment time and tell me he wasn't able to come home to watch the children for me, could I reschedule? This became a logistical nightmare, and truthfully, I missed many of my appointments.

At my sonogram halfway through the pregnancy, David was more nervous than a cat in a room full of rocking chairs. When we got the "all clear" from the doctor and the sonographer, his mood brightened, but only momentarily. Whenever we talked about the baby coming, he would change the subject quickly. I continued to attribute this to his busy schedule and mounting professional pressure as his company expanded and he was working with our church to begin their new building project. He was a busy man indeed.

The baby's due date came and went and my OB insisted on induction. As we drove to the hospital, I began having contractions on my own so I was overjoyed! I chatted and laughed all the way there while David sat stoically in the driver's seat, barely uttering a word.

He's just nervous for me, I thought.

We got to the familiar hospital and the nurses were excited to see us. I saw our pediatrician and we joked as the staff got us checked in. Still...my husband was pensive and quiet.

When our OB walked in, he and David began their usual triathlon talk. After six deliveries and countless medical challenges, my doctor is not only our OB, but a good friend. He and David train together at times and we see him at triathlon races frequently. In the hospital room, Doc took the opportunity to talk racing strategies with David. My delivery was progressing beautifully and finally the time came for me to push.

David held the camera in one hand, my right leg in the other, and snapped photos as Judson made his way into the world. We hadn't discovered the sex of the baby during the pregnancy so it was with great anticipation that I gave that final push and we discovered that Courson had a brother!

"It's a boy, it's a boy!" David and the doctor were beside themselves giddy and laughing. David kept taking photos as I looked down into the lights and saw this massive right hand appear and open up fully to display the longest fingers I had ever seen. While the doctor was busy clamping the cord and wiping the face of the baby, his left hand came into the light and all of a sudden my joy turned to terror.

"His hand, HIS HAND!" I began screaming and shrieking, crying hysterically. In momentary confusion, Doc and David had no idea what I was talking about.

Then they saw it.

A tiny little hand, a thumb tucked into the palm, and four little nubs where his fingers should be.

The photos caught in procession are heart-wrenching. Elated joy on my face turns to fear and tears. My hands cover my mouth instinctively and then I reach for the baby and bring him to my chest, my eyes flooding his face with tears.

What was wrong with my precious son?

David was amazing. His formerly stressed face

during delivery vanished. Now he was covered in pure joy. He grabbed that boy with the umbilical cord still attached, wrapped him in a blanket and said emphatically, "Don't worry sweetie! Look at him! He's just fine! It's *just* his fingers missing! You'll see! He's going to be the greatest quarterback the NFL has ever seen!"

I looked at David like he was crazy. How could he be so happy when our son was just born *missing his fingers*?

David handed me back my little boy all swaddled up. I had chosen the name Judson Worth. I had always adored the name Judson based on the heroic tales of Adoniram Judson the missionary. I loved Worth as a middle name because my father's initials were JW. After I discovered that the name Judson meant "praise" I chose verse 14 from Psalm 139 which talks about a baby being formed in it's mother's womb. As I prayed at that instant holding my new baby boy, I heard the voice of God resound that verse in my mind..."*I will praise you for I am fearfully and wonderfully made...*"(NKJV)

I decided to stick with the name we had already chosen. Even though my heart was breaking and my mind was full of fear, I kept reciting this verse over and over in my mind, telling myself that God does not make mistakes.

Over the next half hour, Dr. Litt witnessed me at my worst and saw my husband at his best. David explained that he knew all along. He knew when I told him months ago in Israel that we were expecting that the baby was a boy and that something would be wrong. He never shared his suspicions with me because he didn't want me to worry... but once he saw that it was only the missing fingers, he was so thankful! Even though over the course of his decades in practice my doctor had seen much worse, far more tragic circumstances, rarely had it been such good friends in the delivery room. He cried too. Consoling me with what he knew and getting specialists to come see the baby as soon as possible, we decided to keep the little hand a secret until we knew more information and could share with friends and family what we understood about the entire issue.

Later that day, our pediatrician visited, and in trying to lighten my mood, he exclaimed my boy was just fine. "He'll probably never play the piano like Beethoven, but other than that he's perfectly healthy."

In true David Reback form, he had a baby grand piano delivered to the house a few weeks later.

"Nobody's gonna tell *my* boy he can't do something!"

God, I love that man.

In the first few months of Judson's life, we went to several specialists and even to the Cleveland Clinic in Ohio. The surgical solutions that most doctors gave had far too many risks that outweighed the benefits. We decided to leave his little "special hand" alone.

I was left to my own imagination.

What had I done to bring this upon my child?

I wasn't faithful in taking my prenatal vitamins. I shouldn't have traveled overseas. I had worked way too many hours in my garden and had my hands in the fertilizers and chemicals far too often. What sins had I ever committed that my child would be punished by missing his fingers? What wrong had I done or what medications had I taken that could have caused this? For six months straight I struggled with sadness and heartbreak thinking of all the challenges my boy would face and how I had somehow brought this upon him. It was an endless cycle of guilt and blame.

Judson was just a cutie pie of a little baby boy who had no idea he was missing any appendages. He played and smiled and giggled all the time! Right around his six-month birthday, the black cloud over me broke and I finally realized: I had done absolutely NOTHING to contribute to Judson's hand.

I began to read all the stories of healing in the Bible and especially about the one where Jesus healed the man with the withered hand. I prayed every night that God would heal his little hand and I fully believed I could walk into the nursery any morning and see four fingers fully formed. My God *could* do that...*certainly* He could.

Then one day I landed on a certain section of Scripture as I was praying.

"Rabbi," his disciples asked Him, "Why was this man born blind? Was it because of his own sins or his parents' sins?"

"It was not because of his sins or his parents' sins," Jesus answered. "This happened so the power of God could be seen in him." (John 9:2-3 NLT)

Man, I held on to that verse and what David had said at the moment of Judson's birth like crazy. I decided to believe God's Word, and what my husband had declared about Judson's future, over the guilt and blame the enemy had been surrounding me with. What if this malformation really was for the glory of God? Who was I to complain or be sad about any of it?

So I stopped praying that his hand would be fixed and started praying that Judson would be used. That was a powerful shift in the moment of my parenting...and one I thought many parents could stand to hear.

How many of us struggle with different challenges our children have? Maybe it's as simple as our child has a difficult time in social settings. Perhaps our child struggles with anxiety. Maybe our daughter has an eating disorder. Our child is given a diagnosis...hyperactivity, ADD, ADHD, bipolar, Crohn's, CANCER. Maybe our child has an addiction...cutting, drugs, pornography...oh Lord, have mercy, the list is endless. The challenges parenting can bring are enough. But parenting a child with any kind of special need, handicap, or diagnosis is difficult on a whole different level. If you have been blessed with healthy children, free of any diagnosis or issues, praise God. But if you have children who struggle physically or emotionally, I am here to tell you, YOU CAN STILL PRAISE GOD.

God does not waste a single hurt, a single challenge, a single struggle in our parenting. Our children may have all kinds of issues, we may be given various diagnoses, but our God is bigger and He will USE IT to His Glory.

He can heal.

He can use.

He can grow us through these difficulties and do something amazing in our families. We have to stop blaming ourselves or listening to the voice of the enemy that tells us we have done something wrong to deserve this punishment. We have to start believing in a God who loves us and will use these challenges to show off His great power. Just like he told his disciples...

"This happened so that God's mighty works might be displayed in him." (John 9:3 CEB)

Believe that God has a work He wants to do in and through your family, regardless of the challenges you are facing, the diagnosis you've been given or the issues your children may struggle with. God just wants to use those things to display the kind of work He can do through all of it!

10.

Power of Belonging

God sets the solitary in families...
Psalm 68:6 NKJV

Judson was about four months old when we got a telephone call from a friend who was a social worker. She had been called by an adoption attorney who was having a difficult time placing a birth mother with an adoptive family.

"This birth mom wants to continue to see the baby several times a year after he is born...would you and David even be *open* to that?" It was a good question indeed, and one that would have to wait, since David was out of town on a mission trip.

When David got back, we met with the social worker and decided to have the birth mom over for dinner. We figured it was worth the risk to explore the idea. Worst-case scenario? We would have spent an evening encouraging a mom who had made the difficult choice of choosing life for an unexpected pregnancy and was further considering adoption. The least we could do was feed her a good steak.

When the evening of her visit arrived, the entire family was excited to meet her. The children welcomed her immediately and she seemed to feel at ease right away. After a hearty meal, David and I put the kids to bed and spent quite a long time talking with this birth mother and the social worker. I don't remember everything we discussed, but I remember the peace in her eyes and the resolve in her decision. Within a short span of time, we were now expecting another son.

Shepherd would be our tenth child. His birth family, all genetic giants, had one member more handsome and beautiful than the next. I remember thinking the moment I laid eyes on his birth mother that whoever got this baby would be getting one beautiful boy.

Within two minutes of his birth, I was proven right. Shepherd, just like his sister Glory Grace, was born with his hair perfectly parted to the side and an adorable face. Big blue eyes, blond hair, and fat little cheeks, he was the picture of perfection! David and I were blessed to spend the forty-eight hours after Shepherd's birth in the hospital with he and big brother Judson in the room together. I was even able to breastfeed them both for a while. In the state of Florida, the birth mother can place her child with an adoptive family and begin to terminate her right to parent at forty eight hours old. I was present for the meeting with the adoption attorney, her assistant, a stenographer, the birth mother, her parents, her aunt, a friend, the social worker and David. Eleven people witnessed the moment this woman handed me her son for an opportunity at a better life. She took a risk betting on us, that we would honor her requests of continued visits and contact. Even though we agreed, legally she had no rights after these papers were signed, and we were not obligated by anything except our conscience to follow through with the agreement. We took a risk on her, hoping that her demands would remain to those stated in our agreement and that she would honor our boundaries and our parenting choices. I've never wanted to hug someone so bad, while simultaneously desiring to run like hell from a room. Our hearts broke as she signed the papers, but our hope with Shepherd quickly filled the sadness. Gut-wrenchingly, I knew she did not have *anything* to fill that emptiness when she left the hospital. Her heartbreak was just beginning.

The first few months were very challenging indeed. The birth mother was trying to deal with an incredible loss. I was busy assimilating this child into our family. At the same time, I felt a responsibility for the emotional well-being of the birth mother, which was extremely difficult. I found myself torn when she would call. I wanted to help her cope with her sadness and be a solid witness for Christ in her life.

I soon learned that it was not my job to disciple my son's birth mom. My job was to be Shepherd's mother. I had to let her go and just stick with our original contact agreement.

Looking back, it was a rough couple of years in trying to work through the relationship with Shepherd's birth family. If it was rough for us, I cannot imagine the struggles they faced. I get a lot of questions about adopting and especially about open adoption.

Is Open Adoption Right for Everyone?

Probably not. David and I were secure in our parenting because we were blessed enough to know what "bonding" really looks and feels like through having our own biological children and also two previous closed adoptions. To be honest, I'm not always sure open adoptions are even the best idea for the birth parents, but I can only speak from my viewpoint as an adoptive mother. Continued contact, especially in those first few weeks and months was difficult on all of us. It felt as though every phone call or visit was like opening up a wound, watching it bleed, and then trying to reapply the old scab when we walked away from one another. I loathed it all, but we held true to our agreement even when drama would flare up...as is likely to happen when you have this many emotions encircling such a sweet baby boy.

It's really difficult to assess whether open adoption is right for an adoptive family or for the birth mom, as experiences, personalities, and circumstances surrounding every adoption are wide and varied. Our open adoption is a beautiful thing now...but it was surely far more challenging than David and I anticipated. I can tell you that through the lens of time and healing, now I wouldn't change a thing. Bringing Shepherd into our family has been the most incredible blessing.

Building Family Identity and Culture

Parents frequently ask me, "*How do I keep my kids*

from worrying so much about what their friends think? How do I keep them from trying to always fit in?" These are valid questions as we witness the powerful desire our children have to fit in.

Wanting to fit in is not necessarily a bad trait. I'm not exactly sure that the desire to belong and identify with a group of fellow friends is even possible to completely eradicate from our code as humans.

What I am about to share with you is something so basic, yet incredibly vital in our family dynamics. Either we take hold of this and become intentional, or we dismiss it and by our decision to not utilize this one facet, we lose major ground in our child replicating our belief systems and values.

Identity

Identity is multifaceted for sure. There's a reason successful companies, churches, big universities and their sports teams have fanatic loyalty. One of those main reasons is identity.

Let's take big university sports teams for example.

Every school has their colors.
Every kid on campus has a flag, a baseball cap, the

bumper sticker, and a half dozen t-shirts. College football season comes and you don't even have to ask where someone went to school, they're wearing it. *Families* can have a color scheme, too! I dress our kids alike because it looks great in photos, helps me keep track of them in a crowd, and makes arguing over what we are going to wear almost a non-event. But the biggest bonus, and I learned this by accident, is that it provides a united front and a *"we belong to each other"* mentality. Sometimes our color schemes will last a year or several years, but you'll always see us coordinating.

Every school has a song.
Everybody sings it at the games and in the bars. *Families can have a song, too!* Our family has a little song list—some of them are the ones we sing every night before bed..."How Great is Our God," "Amazing Grace," and this silly little off tune ditty I made up called "Momma Loves Her Babies." Other songs are our theme songs, like Newsboys' "Wherever We Go, That's Where the Party's At" and Katy Perry's "Unconditional." (And yes, I said *Katy Perry.* Listen to the words of the song...it sure sounds like Jesus talking to me!) But hands down our longest running theme song is another little

tune we made up about being fearless because Jesus loves us. *Sometimes a little song can be hugely powerful.*

Every school's arena has a slogan.
And a nickname. And a tailgate section with its own set of traditions. *Families can have a slogan too!* Our house has a slogan, *"Love Lives Here."* Everyone is welcome. We have people over frequently with the sole intention of making them feel loved. We have traditions that have been etched into our culture and become a part of who we are. Honestly, I mostly stumbled upon these simple strategies, but their effect has been radical.

So I encourage you mama-who's-worried-about-her-kids-wanting-to-fit in...look around your household and into your family. Are there ways you can be intentional about building up a family identity strong enough to lead and guide your children's decisions in making friends or following others? Because what I have discovered is that we can actually build a family culture that other families and children will naturally gravitate toward...and then you will be the influencer in not only your child's life but in the lives of others as well.

Big Business and the Little Family

I've never been to business school, but I believe

that families can learn a lot from how successful businesses are run. One thing that contributes greatly to a thriving business is a strong sense of *unified culture*. Employees who buy into their employer's work environment culture stay longer, work harder, and are their employer's best advertisement. By stark contrast, those companies with detrimental cultures, or sometimes even worse—lack of intentional cultures—have a hard time giving their employees a sense of worth or purpose in their jobs.

I have found the same to be true under my roof. As a family, our shared core belief—that Christ has saved us by grace—and our unique way of presenting the joy of living with faith in that belief, has shaped how we do family. Our family's culture and identity has had the effect of a snowball rolling downhill when it comes to influence and buy-in with our children.

The following are some of our culture characteristics.

We are joyful.
The most common comment I get from by-standers is that our children are so happy. Why wouldn't they be? Yes, a family this size is a lot of work, but if you had sixteen people encouraging you every

day, wouldn't you be happy too? Our culture of encouragement and joy, flowing from a firm foundation in the love and grace of Jesus Christ, is our best advertisement for the King. As His children, we are joyful.

We talk.

And talk. And talk to each other. The meals may only last for an hour, but the talking around the table can last for three. Current events become teaching points, the "why" of what happened and the mindset that leads to decisions is something we discuss all the time. The children often have unique viewpoints and because of our relaxed atmosphere during these discussions, the children feel the freedom to voice their opinions. I wouldn't trade our morning devotionals that follow our mealtimes for anything.

We laugh.

Yes, toddlers and small children can be challenging, but before we lose our patience, we often find the humor. Even when I am getting onto someone, more times than not, I interject humor into the situation. It usually keeps me from using bad words and my (sometimes) loud voice and harsh tone are lessened by the funny joke I throw into the mix.

We use movie lines.
Sounds silly, but a family this much into film can have almost an entire conversation in code. Dozens of movie lines from hundreds of films can be strung together to speak in a different language—no one around us has a clue as to what we are talking about.

We give nicknames.
My dad used to do this all the time to my friends, so I guess it came naturally to me. The children have nicknames, their friends have nicknames, the neighbors, and especially, the **boys**. Boys who have shown interest in any of my girls all get nicknames. And that is DEFINITELY a hat tip to my father. *He LOVED to do that to me.*

We are athletic.
David is awesome at triathlons, I am just into fitness for fun. The kids get a perfect mix of competitiveness and cheerleading. The physical side of our family has contributed so much to our character training and spiritual lessons that we would not be the same without this part of our culture.

We dress alike...
or at least coordinate. Sounds unimportant, but it brings simplicity and unity. When we had three small children, it was just easier for me to dress them all the same. But now that we have added to our family through adoption, dressing alike has contributed greatly to our cohesiveness.

We have a "You Can Do Anything" mentality.
We never cast doubt on their dreams, we never throw water on their fire. The children want to do big things in life. Being so young, they rarely realize how difficult these visions or purposes will be. But it's not my job as a parent to throw their desires under a bus. My job is to ready them for a life of near backbreaking challenges and overcome-able obstacles, all the while speaking purpose, faith, and "you can do it!"

As you can see, some of these are philosophical, some of them are silly, some are practical. But they all add up to a culture that is uniquely ours and gives the family identity and distinctions. I challenge you to observe what things make up your family's culture. What things would you like to see a part of your family's culture? What things would you like to see removed? Write them down! The role it plays can be far more significant than you imagine as the children age. Indeed, your family's culture can be the strongest defense against peer pressure and their biggest offense in leadership among their peer group.

More on Dressing My Children Alike

When I had my oldest three daughters in less than three years, I began dressing them alike. Truthfully, it made it easy to dress them for outings, and it always photographed nicely. David liked the idea because if I was not home, he knew exactly what to have them wear. All three dresses would be on the same hanger. Brainless wardrobing for a daddy who, let's just say, is not the most talented at putting together outfits.

Dressing alike made arguments about clothing non-existent. I went shopping once a year and purchased seven to nine outfits for each child that all coordinated. After shopping, I usually consigned or gave away what was left from the previous year. The girls loved the positive remarks they received about how they were dressed. Since David and I coordinated, or at least wore the same color as the children, it never seemed odd to my oldest girls to wear matching clothing.

By the time Daly Kay was ten, we had adopted

two children, one boy and one girl. At this point, dressing alike became very important. This was not just for the sake of ease. Our newest daughter, Liberty, didn't exactly look like us genetically. So when people would look a bit quizzically at us, it was obvious she belonged to our family because she matched her sisters. By then, dressing alike, or coordinating outfits, had become our trademark. It was a part of our family identity.

This only grew in importance as we added more children through adoption. Dressing alike made their sense of belonging to our family seamless. Of course, I know there are many contributing factors to my adopted children's confidence, but I really believe that something as simple as clothing matters.

Sometimes people are amazed that my oldest girls all match...even at twenty, eighteen, and seventeen. But you know what? Next time you see a group of three teenage girls together, look closely. Likely, they are all wearing the same thing, too. Same cut off jeans, same flip-flops, same black tank tops, same handbags, same hairstyle. In the effort to conform, to try to not stand out, or to please their friends or feel as though they belong to their particular group, they dress alike. That's how they "identify" what group they belong to...

surfer, cowboy, punk, alternative, or hipster. Our children do the same thing. They identify themselves as Rebacks by how they dress, among a host of other characteristics and traits.

Most noticeably at first glance, the manner in which they dress draws attention...*in the right way.* By now, they have come to really get a kick out of the wide-eyed look people give our family when they see us coming. If I had a dime for every time someone asked to take a picture of us, David could retire. In any case, whether you dress your children alike or not, it's important to remember that your child will be identified by how they dress. People often make their first assumptions about your child based on what they see. If your child is older and making the decision of what to wear, they are identifying themselves with their manner of dress. In many cases, lots of loaded arguments about how to dress, especially with girls, could be avoided with some solid, intentional training about clothing and its implications from an early age.

What I like about how my oldest girls dress is that even though they wear the same outfit, their styles are still different. Their haircut, makeup, and jewelry all reflect their personalities. You couldn't have three girls with more differing physical shapes either. So the dresses may match, but they are worn differently by each girl. And I love that.

So that's why we dress alike. Lots of times people will remark as we go by, "Oh, look! It's the Von Trapp family from *Sound of Music!*" And Daly Kay always responds, "We have more than twice as many kids as they did!"

While I have focused on dressing alike quite a bit in this chapter, it is just one of the ways we are cohesive as a family. All the children are on a swim team. Everyone does triathlons. We all sit together at church. Once a week we have a movie night. Do some of the children develop their own interests and hobbies? Certainly! But even then, we will all go to the play or the football game together to support that one child. Building family identity and culture is very much about cohesiveness and being a strong support system for every member of the family. Think of some ways that your family can develop its own identity and culture as well as build cohesiveness. Make a list of activities you commonly do together and see how those can be used to make your family stronger.

11.

Never Say No

Shout joyfully to the Lord, all the earth.
Serve the Lord with gladness;
Come before him with joyful singing.
Psalm 100:1-2 NASB

Many times people assume that I have continued to bear children because my pregnancies must be easy and enjoyable. While I have not struggled severely with nausea during the early months, and during postpartum blues I fare pretty well (except for days five through twelve...those days are just full of tears), I can assure you that several pregnancies have had their difficulties. Ransom's in particular.

It's Not Always Easy

It was July 4th weekend and we were staying with

some friends who also had a large family. On my way downstairs for breakfast, I slipped and cracked my head so loudly that everyone in the house came running. I had also knocked my hip and was sore for days. I was six months along with Ransom and showing. After a few minutes of lying down on a bed with some ice on my head, we continued with the weekend's festivities.

For several weeks my hip and head hurt, but I figured that soreness was to be expected with that big of a fall. I kept my activity level normal and assumed that over time, whatever the problem was would just resolve itself.

One particularly long and busy day, I returned home late in the evening after errand running and dinner with a friend. When I pulled into my driveway and parked my car, I found it impossible to get up out of the sitting position in the driver's seat. I just couldn't move. I had excruciating pain in my pelvic region, and I sat immobilized trying to call David from my cell phone in the driveway. All to no avail...my dear husband was sleeping soundly. Finally with no other option, I began crawling from the car, up the steps of my front stoop, and to the door...praying all along that none of my neighbors would drive by thinking I was inebriated! Fully laid out on the stoop, I banged on the front door until my husband opened it, completely dazed and confused. Sudden fear gripped his face —what in the world was I doing sprawled out on the doormat?

When I explained my severe pain he immediately called my OB. After a few minutes the doctor rightly concluded that my pelvic bone had most likely separated in the front. He asked me to come in the following morning and upon examination he handed me the verdict: mostly bed rest for the remaining three-plus months of pregnancy and there really wasn't anything that could be done to relieve the pain.

I came home that morning and wept on my couch. Daly Kay was thirteen and we had ten children in the home. Four of them were under two years old. David was busy with three real estate offices and a general contracting business. It wasn't likely he would be able to slow down enough to be of much help. How on earth was I going to maintain this household, homeschooling and my sanity while being mostly immobile?

After I had somewhat composed myself, I sat down with the children old enough to understand what was wrong with mommy. I told them that I realized this meant a lot of extra work and responsibility for each of them, but that at the end of this trial we would be stronger as a family. Over the next couple of days, I reworked our routine and the children's responsibilities and within a few more days we had adjusted pretty well.

Upon recommendation from my doctor, we purchased a walker. Although I hated to use it, bearing my weight on anything other than my pelvis was preferable to the pain of being in almost any position except lying down. Sitting was actually the worst. Whenever someone would knock at the door, we would hide the walker since we decided to keep my physical restraints and challenges a private family matter. Friends and family were already skeptical of our choice to continue adding to our family, and this latest setback would just be fodder for gossip and criticism...two things, that in my emotional and physical state, I did not need.

Cabin fever soon became my biggest challenge as I hardly left home, and yet my concentrated effort on the children reaped many positive results. Without a mom able to physically do much, each of my older children had to really step it up. Initially, of course, it was frustrating. But over time we developed systems where I could still be effective. On cleaning days the children would take pictures of their rooms and show them to me in my bed, and I could still give congratulations or constructive criticisms. The big girls would assign a sister to me each day as my "helper" who would be my hands and feet around the house. I still shed tears from physical pain and did plenty of crying from trying to maintain "normal" life while being so constrained, but I was learning and growing and so were the children.

Three weeks before his due date, I went into labor. Ransom was born eight pounds, eleven ounces after one push with virtually no pelvis to slow down his decent through the birth canal. A bruise, forehead to chin, formed down his entire face from the broken bone. Without a proper squeeze through the birth canal from the pelvic bones, his lungs didn't get the proper pressure to release the amniotic fluid from pregnancy. Oddly enough, we first noticed his breathing was labored because he made this little sing-songy sound as he exhaled. When a nurse in the room heard my mother exclaim how it sounded as though Ransom was singing, it signaled that something was wrong. Within ten minutes after his birth he was rushed into the Neonatal Intensive Care Unit. After three days of careful observance and his lungs clearing out the fluid while being on supplemental oxygen, he made a wonderful recovery.

My broken pelvis could now begin to heal. Family and friends were finally made aware of our private struggle. My big girls were happy to see mommy getting better by wearing a brace meant to bring the pelvic bones back together. By six weeks postpartum my pelvis was mostly repaired. We had made it!

I share this story with you not to elicit pity, but to hopefully encourage those of you who have had or will endure physical challenges during pregnancy. These limitations can be heartbreaking and beyond frustrating, but they are meant to strengthen us and bring our family closer together. While initially I was distraught and felt hopeless and helpless, I had to decide to believe that my God had chosen this challenge for me and therefore He had to have a way through it. In the end, it turned my oldest daughters into far more capable and responsible young ladies and forced me to focus solely on my family while I was relegated to staying mostly within my four walls.

So, you see that my pregnancies have not always been easy, but they have all been worth it. Even the difficulties...while they were unwanted at the time, today I wouldn't have it any other way.

Ransom the Rockstar

Ransom began operating through life on the loudest volume. His cries were loud. His squeals of delight were louder. By the time he began speaking, we were constantly reminding him to *speak softer*, PLEASE, to absolutely no avail.

His favorite baby toys were instruments, and if it wasn't an instrument, he made it into one. When we did family praise and worship, he was the most visibly moved by the music. "LOUDER, MAMA!" is all he could say when we were in the car rocking out.

Then, every week, starting at about the age of three, he began trying to sneak an instrument into Sunday school. For a month running, I pulled harmonicas, flute recorders, maracas, and tambourines out of his pockets as he exited the car to go to church. Finally, he tried to make it past me with a CD hidden under his shirt.

"Ransom! What are you doing? Why is it every week you are trying to sneak something into Sunday school?"

In a fit of tears, he responded completely exasperated, "But, Momma! They don't do praise and worship in my class! And we NEED to praise Jesus!"

Right then, it struck me. This kid, with his beautiful, raspy voice and volume control issues, was destined to sing. A praise and worship leader in the making. And suddenly a lot of the puzzle pieces came together.

I have had lots of parents ask me *how* we know what each kid is made to do. We saw Ransom's different traits, tendencies, and characteristics and began to string them together. Then we started to speak it over him in faith. We were no longer annoyed at his continual singing, and for the most part, we left his volume alone. We exposed him to different kinds of music, and Daly Kay is teaching him piano. At church, we began bringing him into big service with us so he could enjoy the praise and worship. Most importantly, we shared this purpose with others, and eventually, that led to a really special experience for him.

Glimpses of Glory

Ransom listens to worship music constantly and watches his favorite praise and worship team every week on TV.

Eventually, one summer our family visited the church we had been watching. While there, my little future praise and worship leader got the opportunity to stand on the same stage we saw weekly on television. He got to sing, microphone and all, to an empty auditorium filled with thousands of seats. By giving him this daunting task, we were showing him how much we believe in him. When he got to personally speak with the worship team he so admires and sing a few bars for them, their encouragement was powerful. And when one of the worship leaders hugged him and said, "Are you the one who is going to be a worship leader? You gonna sing with me on stage one day?" the poor kid nearly blacked out.

Ransom's story sheds a new light on a familiar Scripture. "Train up a child in the way he should go,"(Proverbs 22:6 NKJV) sounds to me like there is a way to train a child and it is paramount that the parent should know what direction this kid is meant to go. Most parents I know use this verse to speak about morality and obedience, but those two things *should* be a given, and they don't really have much to do with direction. The purpose our child was created to fulfill will definitely need some direction, training, education, preparation, and faith. As a parent there is nothing more inspiring, nothing more powerful, not a single thing more rewarding than seeing your child begin to walk in that purpose.

This job of parenting can be exhausting, but all it takes is a few moments of clarity, like what I've explained with little Ransom, to bring fresh wind into our sails and spur us on to prevail against all odds. I like to call these precious moments

Glimpses of Glory.

These instances give us little hints and small clues into the future of our children. They may have to do with a talent or calling, like Ransom and his love of music and volume, or they may include character traits uniquely inside of the child. My son, Judson, is a great hugger. His affections can lighten a burden, bring joy and relief, or calm a new friend. Ryli has a sense of humor. When she lights up a room with her comedic remarks, I see a glimpse of how God will use her to bring joy to hurting and needy people.

What happens if we are wrong? What if Ransom wasn't created to be a worship leader after all? Worst-case scenario? He has been exposed to fine music and has felt the devoted belief of his parents and siblings that he can accomplish whatever great purpose he sets out to do. And along the way, we will have been musically entertained.

But I'm not wrong. Ransom is going to sing. Beautifully. And now you have one example of how the Lord loves to lead us in our parenting and guide us in the joyful scavenger hunt that is finding your child's purpose and pursuing it passionately.

Never Say No

Have you ever read a biography or watched a movie and found yourself inspired by someone else's accomplishments? Have you ever looked on at another person's life that seemed so fulfilled and wondered how they got there? Biographies are some of my favorite books, because through them, I get to walk a while in someone's shoes and find out how they made it as far as they did. The one thing they all have in common?

A steady belief that anything is possible.

Our children will be told "no" hundreds of times in their lives. They will be told "never" by people they respect and hope to emulate. There will be rejection letters and stinging moments of embarrassment or pain from friends, peers, and even professors and coaches. But one place they should never face any of that is from their parents.

Let me give you a personal example from my own childhood...

As a child, I was into dance: tap, ballet, jazz, and gymnastics. I simply loved ballet. I began at age four and danced until I was nineteen years old. I *don't* think I was particularly gifted, as I never moved onto pointe and was never given a solo or part to play of any importance...but in my mind, I was brilliant at it. I loved the music, the recitals, and I adored watching my ballet teacher move so fluidly through the classroom.

When I was about nine, I felt like I had really come a long way in dance. Thinking myself to be some sort of prodigy, I was elated when my ballet teacher announced that this year's recital would be on a large stage downtown and televised. I went home that night and told my parents I was going to ask for a solo performance.

Now my parents had to know how this was going to end. I mean, they loved me and enjoyed my performances for them in the living room, but surely they knew I was not superiorly talented.

They never let on.

"No harm in asking," they told me. "Go right on ahead and ask. You never know!"

So I prepared a little audition dance on my own, in case the owner of the studio asked me to perform on the spot. I wrote a letter explaining my vast experience of five years and how I knew I was ready to be put in a solo on television. My parents watched all this happen over the course of a week, and on Friday, I approached the owner of the studio.

Of course, she told me no.

And yes, I was disappointed.

But that is not the issue. Being turned down by

the owner of the studio (and believe me, she had GOOD reason) was the first of *many* rejections I can recall in the thirty years since. However, my dreams were not rejected by my parents. They encouraged me throughout that week even knowing all along the woman would turn me down.

And what did I learn?

Give it a chance, put your best effort out there, and see what happens.

With hard work, anything is possible.

And without at least asking, you'll never get the opportunity!

In my own parenting, I have learned to never discourage a dream. And believe me, my kids have dreamt big and in many cases their vision and calling has been something I may ponder with a quaking heart. Over time I have seen that it is my job to listen, encourage, pray, and *never say no*.

There are so many times as a parent we must say no (no, you can't go there...no, such and such is not a good friend to hang around with...no, I don't care if everyone else is doing it, you're not!). In the area of the desires of our child's heart— the things they want to accomplish with their lives—we should never say no to those precious thoughts, dreams, and aspirations. In fact, we should speak of them as though they already are.

Just like we did with Ransom, call it out in faith. Speak it encouragingly over your children, and watch as they begin to see themselves in light of those hopes and dreams.

Never say no.

Because with God, all things are possible.

One of our favorite Ransom quotes came as I was writing this book. When I discussed this chapter with him, he informed me that at his age (six) he has learned three important things: Never give up, never quit, and never stop using your cuteness power.

Yes, my boy has us pretty smitten with his adorableness, but really, the understanding that perseverance pays off is already instilled. Ransom has always been relentless. When he was a toddler in his crib asking for something before we turned out the light at bedtime, denying him did not stop the asking. While this can be challenging in a child, as an adult and channeled the right way, this character trait is actually a great strength. As much as possible, my husband and I try and see those things about our children that can drive us nuts through a new lens. How might this character trait be used positively? Directed and trained the right way, could this actually be a benefit to them? Why might God have woven this into them? With this new viewpoint, we can see that not all traits that we perceive as negative must be trained or disciplined out of them. Sometimes these negatives can actually be turned and used for good.

One of my favorite Glimpses of Glory happened with Ransom's big brother Judson. I had just had baby Verity and my postpartum recovery involved a spinal sac tear, which gave me a migraine headache that lasted seven days straight. I made it to Judson's last football game of the season and stood near the end zone for the final drive of the game. The ball snapped, Judson caught it, and ran toward the end zone at Mach1! The entire time his eyes were locked on mine, his smile was huge, and with every ounce of his being, his body and soul were radiating, "Do you see me, Mama? DO YOU SEE ME DOING THIS!?!?"

I just laughed, cried, and melted all at once. I had barely been able to stand up for the last week, and now I was jumping, screaming, yelling, and crying...it was a magical Glimpse of Glory...a glimpse into his future and a pat on the back from Above.

If we follow these Glimpses of Glory and give our children opportunities by considering how we can Never Say No, one day, it may very well be a biography about the life of our child that inspires someone else to greatness!

12.

Love Is Spelled
T-I-M-E

*Now faith is the substance of things hoped for,
the evidence of things not seen.*

Hebrews 11:1 NKJV

Sojourner Hope was born just ten short weeks after Ransom. We had known about her for many months before she came into the world. David and I prayed her adoption would go smoothly. By the time she was born, my broken pelvis had healed nicely and little Ransom was feeding and sleeping on a pretty good routine. I was truly excited about this little girl coming into our family. We named her after our journey of hope through prayer to bring her into our lives. We met our attorney a few blocks away from the hospital where Soji was born and laid eyes on her for the first time.

She came to us in the car seat we had given the attorney, dressed in nothing but a stained hospital newborn T-shirt and a diaper. Her head full of hair and fat little cheeks were remarkable, but what was most noticeable was the frown this baby was wearing.

We have all seen babies who smile as newborns during a sleep state and many grandmothers will tell you it's just gas. But this little girl had a distinct frown. "Soji," as we came to call her, had a generally unhappy look and feel about her, even as I took in her face for the first time. We brought her into our car full of her new siblings, who were completely overjoyed to finally see the baby they had been praying for, and one by one, many of them remarked about her tiny, sad face.

Joyfulness Can Be Taught

We took her home and loved on her endlessly.

We bathed her with care, fed her bottles with love, dressed her adorably and snuggled her constantly. Still, by three and four months of age, she had yet to smile.

Tickling, kissing, blowing raspberries, and loving on her constantly gave us no return happiness. Even though she rarely cried, little Soji never smiled.

So David and I began to pray. We started to call her our "Happy Soji." We talked about how pretty her little smile was, even though we had yet to see it, and kept talking about her as though she was already happy.

I would love to tell you that there was an immediate turn around. I wish I could say that I was not scared of her emotional state or well-being, especially given the circumstances surrounding her adoption. Frequently I feared what kind of future suffering she may endure because of her sadness. But still we kept calling out joy in faith.

Finally at eighteen months of age, we began to see a turn around. Even though we still had to work pretty hard to get a smile from Soji, she could and would smile. She began to mimic an attempt at laughter. We praised any small gesture toward exhibiting joy, and I am glad to say that now, by six years of age, she is known as a happy and joyful child. She loves to perform for us and has quite a knack for acting. My constant prayer over her these last six years has been that wherever she would travel (Sojourn), she would bring the Hope of Jesus. I don't yet know what God is going to do with this adorable little muffin, but I do know that wherever He leads her, she will go with joy. She may not have been born happy, but joy can be taught, folks.

It would have been easy to label her unhappy and even to give into that sense, because perhaps, there really was something to the circumstances surrounding the things she heard and felt prenatally while her birth mother struggled with whatever challenges led her to place her child for adoption. However, David and I chose to believe in a joyful outcome for Soji's overall attitude, because we believe it is God's good pleasure to make His beloved children smile.

I'll also tell you that while Judson (#9) was a baby who was easy to get a smile from, he was also given to anger. He could stare down a church nursery volunteer and make her wonder what on earth this baby was brooding about! There came a point when David and I realized this and began to work consistently on encouraging him when he was happy and smiling. We would also get onto him when he began to give that "evil eye" and have a menacing face. It wasn't that we did not allow him to be angry or frustrated, but we simply did not want a boy to grow up angry without a cause. Over time, Judson's fretting face completely disappeared and now no one who knows him would characterize him as angry. Fiercely competitive, maybe...but not angry. And for that I thank God.

So let's not let fears and predispositions take charge of our children's destinies. Whatever impossible attitude you are facing with your children or in your own heart, it is all overcomeable. Let's call out the traits in faith that we desire for our children. Like the Syro-Phoenician woman struggling with her demon possessed daughter in Matthew chapter 15 verse 28, let's hear the Lord say, "O woman, great *is* your faith! Let it be to you as you desire." (NKJV) He sees our struggles. He hears our prayers. The Lord of creation delights to answer our biggest requests. And I'm believing with you!

Love Is Spelled T-I-M-E

I went to boarding school at a young age, and my parents traveled extensively while I was away. Families of the friends I made at school had to fill in a lot of gaps. One mother who took the time and effort to pour into me as a young lady was Liz Moore.

Liz was the mom of my dearest friend Beth. She was beautiful, head to toe. Her hair was always done, she was dressed to the nines, and full of Southern grace and grit. She lived by example and preached with her life more often than with her words.

Liz worked tirelessly to help her husband's business, her daughters with schoolwork, and also served ministering to her church and charities. But the priorities never got confused. I vividly remember a conversation with Liz when I was sixteen years old. Over the years, these words have guided me as a mom:

"Lyette (said with three syllables instead of two—"LEE-eu-tt"—because as a Texan, it really does take three) just remember, lots of women love to do ministry, but they leave behind the first ministry of their family. Later they wonder why their children don't love church and refuse to serve or follow Jesus."

There is always someone, somewhere, asking us for something. Can we help here? Can we volunteer there? Just for a few hours? Can we please serve just once a month? Can we give a little time to this charity, this ministry?

I also know it is possible to do some of these things. I have definitely served my church and my community. We have taken some of our children on mission trips. We have served as a family to those in our community in need of help. However, I have to make sure that none of my other responsibilities go undone because of said service, and that my children are not in any way put aside. Because, you see, service can sometimes be a clever disguise for running away from issues we don't want to face at home, in our marriage, our children, or even ourselves. Serving can become a placater of purpose, a side street to sanity.

I recently counseled a wife whose husband told her at their holiday dinner table that he was done with their marriage...and he left! He was tired of all her running about and ignoring his needs. Thank you, sweet Jesus, they have since mended many of their issues. This man was ready to leave his family because of the hopelessness he felt in part due to his wife's inability to say no when someone or some organization asked for help.

This reminded me of what Jesus said, "You will always have the poor among you, but you will not always have me." (John 12:8 NIV)

Perhaps I am just super sensitive to this issue right now. I know I won't always have all my children under one roof. I understand that our days are limited to be together and so every moment spent apart had better darn well be worth it. There will always be the poor and needy, but there will not always be another Friday movie night with everyone. The Saturdays with nothing to do but enjoy a sunny day at the beach with every family member will, sooner rather than later, involve plane tickets and months of planning and scheduling.

Prioritize. Enjoy every minute you can together. They grow up faster than you think and then...you can serve until you drop.

Relying on and hoping for "quality time" when as a family there is not copious amounts of "quantity time" spent together, is an ineffective and risky parenting strategy. Lots of parents say the buzzwords "quality time" to me when they are trying to justify large amounts of time spent apart as a family...all members running fifty-six different directions with the intention of doing everything every member of the family wants to do.

But here's a newsflash folks...quality time doesn't happen when you want it to. It happens when you have copious amounts of quantity time together. Quality time—those precious moments that overtake you and fill your child's cup with a smidgen of understanding about how much you love them—happen when you least expect it. You can't engineer that with two hours at Chuck E. Cheese's. You can't manufacture those memories with an hour at the park. These moments can't be pushed on a relationship. They are the natural phenomenon of spending your life really WITH someone.

So slow down.

Milking the Moment

The children were all piling into the car after a neighborhood Easter egg hunt. It was hot. After a rain, the sun was baking all the moisture out of the ground and David was struggling to get the pram back into the van. Easter baskets full of junk and choking-hazard-sized toys were littering the entire inside of a vehicle that two of my children had just worked hard to clean. Everyone was starving for lunch. I held five-month-old baby Verity as I walked toward the door of the van to buckle her in.

But I stopped five feet from my intended destination. Little Verity had molded into my body and was gently blowing raspberries on my neck. Cooing and humming, she was hugging me so tightly. One by one, the older children emerged from the van to witness the spectacle of sweetness. As I cradled her little head in my hands and hugged her right back, David walked up to see what all the "oooo-ing and awwww-ing" was about.

"We're not going anywhere, are we?"

He knew...when a moment like this happens, I will milk it for every second I can. Hot and sweaty, I was sunburnt from three hours spent outside. Desperately wanting lunch because I had been too busy getting everyone ready that morning and forgot to eat breakfast, I overcame the hunger to remember quickly...these moments don't last forever.

I want to remind you time and again how quickly childhood flies by and you find yourself looking at an adult instead of a toddler.

Keep your eyes and hearts open for those tender moments that can surprise you and build your relationship with your child into a priceless edifice of Christ's love.

Enjoy every single second of each sweet hug, adorable question or comment, or snuggle before naptime. Don't be in such a rush to move on to the next event on your agenda that you miss the biggest way you can give and receive love to your child...whether they are tiny or full grown!

That extra five minutes spent in the parking lot will never be remembered by baby Verity. But the way I loved on her will most certainly be remembered by my older children who watched their momma melt and enjoy the precious memory of cuddling while a baby kissed on her.

Tucking Them In and Teaching Them to Trust

One momma wrote me to tell me about a sweet

and silly conversation she had with her adorable three-year-old before bed. She asked him what his favorite part of the day was, and he answered "macaroni and cheese." She snuggled in and began to ask how she could pray for him. That little darling went on and on about all kinds of things. Nothing very deep or masterful about some desire to grow in an everlasting relationship with the Creator of the universe...he is only three! I submit something way more important was happening.

This little guy was opening up to his mom. His mom was taking the time to ask questions and listen to the seemingly silly and meaningless ramblings of a tired three-year-old.

One day, he won't be three anymore. He will be thirteen. Since I know this momma is wise, she will still be there, bedside late at night, talking with this exhausted middle-schooler. Over the years of discussing macaroni and cheese and the neighbor's dog, he will have begun to open up to her about the struggles he is having with friends. Or those beautiful, frightening creatures called girls. She will have won his heart and his trust with listening to hours of mundane things so that when the time comes for the important issues, she will have proven herself trustworthy and caring.

And at nineteen, he'll call late at night from

college. He will have learned she is a safe place to go to. He'll know she's up late at night anyhow, because even his last year of high school, she was always there to listen to him ramble on into the early hours of the morning. His questions and the challenges he faces are now life altering decisions, but he will know where to go with every issue.

Moms and dads, the last few minutes before bed are when the child's heart is most vulnerable. Tuck them in...every night. Speak your prayers and hopes for them out loud over them while you swipe the hair from their forehead. Tell them they are beautiful, precious, loved, handsome, and the most important thing under your roof. Watch their eyes sparkle and their hearts open wide to share with you their secret hopes and dreams. Develop that trust so that they keep coming to you and talking over the things that trouble them. Sometimes those last conversations of the day run late into the night, but the most important thing is that we are talking things through. How many parents complain their children won't open up, that they won't talk?

I "tuck" this little treasure into Soji's chapter because an important part of teaching her joy was bringing trust into her heart by the simple day-to-day action of tucking her in. Whatever unsettling feelings were rattling around in that little child's head, each night we replaced a bit of that unhappiness with love and trust. Over time we rebuilt her mindset. It was not an "overnight" success but it was an every night effort.

Tuck them in. No matter how long it has been since you have done so or how old your child is. Teach them love and teach them to trust you one goodnight kiss at a time.

13.

The Gift of a Strong-Willed Girl

*For whatever is born of God overcomes the world.
And this is the victory that has overcome the
world—our faith.*

1 John 5:4 NKJV

Crickie is our thirteenth child. Convinced I was having a boy, I arrived at the hospital with everything in blue and only had a boy's name chosen! Quite on the fly, as the doctor asked me her name, I responded, "Victory Rose." David's paternal grandfather had passed away about a year before and his name was Victor. Being such a competitive family, I thought Victory was a beautiful and feminine alternative. Scripturally, I realized that our only real chance at victory in life came because our Savior rose from the grave, and the two words sounded lovely together.

Crickie became her nickname because her sweet older brother Ransom couldn't actually say Victory...it came out more like "Crickory"...which shortened to Crickie. It fits her perfectly.

Blond hair, wildly waving in the wind, Crickie runs everywhere. I don't remember her ever just walking. Addicted to tic-tacs and boldly taking after those siblings who display a strong sense of will, she has all of us wrapped around her little finger.

Even after thirteen children, there are still things we are learning through parenting little Crickie. One of my favorite examples happened a few months ago.

Crickie had been given an American Girl doll by my mother for Christmas. She loved dressing and undressing her doll and took special care every naptime and nighttime to put her dolly into pajamas. Daly Kay had told her that dolly's clothing might get damaged if she slept in anything other than pj's, so Crickie was diligent to listen and follow her older sister's advice...especially since Daly Kay had been sweet enough to let Crickie use some of Daly's doll dresses that she had saved from years ago. This was indeed a privilege and one that little sister Crickie did not want to lose.

It was naptime. We were all tired. Bliss had been given the job of getting Crickie, Soji, and Stone ready for naps while we tidied up lunch. She got Stone and Soji into bed and after a search for Crickie, discovered her deep in the closet redressing her dolly.

"Bedtime Crickie! This is not time to dress dolly!" Crickie protested trying to explain her dilemma, but Bliss was frustrated and just began to demand that Crickie listen immediately and get into bed.

I was in the sunroom reading to Ransom, and could hear what had begun as a slight protest quickly escalate into World War III. It sounded like Bliss was forcibly removing a limb from the way that Crickie was screaming at her! Unable to discern exactly what was being said or why, soon the ear splitting noise drew nearer as Bliss dragged little Crickie into the sunroom and demanded I deal with her since she was obviously beyond reason and had lost any shred of self control.

"Whoa whoa whoa whoa, little mustang! What's going on here?" I asked Crickie.

Crickie's face was a mix of anger and fear. What she tried to explain through sobs and gasps was that she was simply trying to put her dolly's pajamas on when Bliss came in forcing her to go to bed.

"That's right!" said Bliss. "I told you it was bedtime and you needed to listen to me!"

Crickie began to get worked up all over again and I couldn't quite understand what was so vitally important about dolly having on pajamas. From Bliss's perspective it seemed like Crickie was just trying to delay the inevitable naptime, but all this fuss added up to way more than just a stall tactic.

After dismissing Bliss and talking it through for several minutes, I finally came to understand what the uproar was about. Crickie took her job as a new mommy to dolly very seriously and really wanted to treat Daly Kay's doll clothes with care since it was such a big deal to be given access to them. Not putting pajamas on dolly at naptime was tantamount to *neglect* in Crickie's eyes and could very well cost her the privilege of using Daly Kay's clothes if anything happened to even one doll dress.

I finally understood what the problem was. This was not a stall tactic, and it wasn't a temper tantrum. This was a misunderstanding of gargantuan proportions.

Crickie was right. The doll needed pajamas.

I tell you this little story because it illustrates

what can so often happen in our homes if we don't take the time to stop and ask questions during a meltdown. In this case, Bliss was the one not listening but there have been hundreds of times when I was the guilty person. Crickie had a good reason to be upset, but to a tired teenager just ready for some quiet in the afternoon, no reason mattered.

This incident with Crickie serves as a vital reminder. There are plenty of times that toddlers and young ones have meltdowns because they are tired. There are lots of times that they throw fits because they truly do need discipline. What is also critical to remember is that there are frustration tantrums that can escalate quickly because the adult or caregiver in the situation has no real clue as to what is at the bottom of the unrest.

Take the time to discern the difference.

"Be quick to listen, slow to speak and slow to become angry." (James 1:19 NIV)

Learning to listen is a skill worth acquiring as a parent. Sometimes the hardest part is learning to listen for what is *not* being said. Learning to listen and not just jump into teaching mode or preaching mode, but instead learning to draw out the child and ask more questions so that we can better understand where they are coming from, takes time and practice. Admittedly, this truth took time for me to learn.

When the child grows up knowing we are able to listen and willing to help them work through issues, they will continue to open up to us and share with us their most troubling concerns, their deepest desires, and biggest dreams.

Two-year-olds generally don't need a lot of conversation deciphering their deepest issues (hear the sarcasm) but as they grow, please remember this little story about Crickie. Remember why she was so upset, and think to ask questions, listen carefully, and respond slowly. As they grow, your child will know who to trust and where to go when they need a listening ear and solid direction.

The Benefit of a Strong-Willed Child

I can't count the number of times I have been asked if any of my children are strong-willed. Many times I am tempted to respond, "Is there any other kind?" In truth, while many of mine were born with a stubborn streak (apple doesn't fall far from the tree, I guess) I have a particular few who are just amazingly strong.

Willful.

Think...*titanium.*

I'll be honest and say that as wee ones, these kinds of kids can be a handful. They don't give in, they don't give up. They will embarrass you as a parent and humble you in ways (in front of a crowd during an infamous meltdown) that you never even saw coming. I was about five years into my parenting before I could actually laugh about it. Now, with twenty years experience and fifteen children I can tell you: strong-willed kids rock my world in all the right ways.

Strong-willed children have an innate need to know if you really mean what you say. They never just take your word at face value but they must see for themselves if what you are telling them is true.

You tell a strong-willed child not to do something, and they have to do it. As a parent, we can get very frustrated and think, "Why can't this child just do as I tell them???" But many times, parents fail to see that this characteristic alone should be enough to make us respect and admire this child's tenacity.

Because in the long run, we really don't want our child to just accept "whatever" as truth. We would never say we just want our child to grow up and take anyone's word for anything. We want them to know, own, and search out matters for themselves. We want to raise the kind of child who knows the truth and is able to influence others about what truth is.

"It is the glory of God to conceal a matter; to search out a matter is the glory of kings." (Proverbs 25:2 NIV)

You see, as this Proverb explains, learning to search out a matter, trying the rules and discovering boundaries and truth is actually a great leadership quality. While it may be mind-bending for the parent of a child whose strong will is so intent on discovering if we *really* mean what we say, if we *really* know what is best...ultimately, once this kid has been won over and convinced, you have a child who will be a banner carrier for the truth. They will wave their freak flag for Jesus loud and proud and convince multitudes of others to do the same because of their own self-won discoveries.

All that fight...all that verve...focused in the right direction...is what will make that strong-willed child into an amazing leader. We will be glad they never just took what we said and accepted it. They have to fight it out in their own mind, argue things into truth for themselves. Once they have "bought what we are selling," they will be the biggest defender, the biggest advocate for how we do family, how we educate, and how we choose to live. A strong-willed child is a great and powerful blessing, because you see, they will never follow. They will only lead. The need then, as a parent, is to train them to lead well, and to train them to lead others to Jesus and the joy that living in His Word brings.

So those parents struggling with "strong-willed" children: rejoice! You have been given a great opportunity to pour into a future world changer. Don't dare to complain about the child who is so tough! Stay the course, and you will never have to worry about them falling away or being lured into trouble. They will be leading the charge in the right direction, because leading is all they know how to do. It's the only way they know how to be. Training isn't easy, but it is so well worth it. If I can convince parents that the inner strength of our children is an asset, not an insult (to our authority or our ego) then this book will have made a difference in the lives of all the families blessed enough to have a strong-willed child.

Love on those tough nuts...and one day they will be a mighty oak of strength.

Bossy Is a Bad Word

I have rarely heard parents complain about their

strong-willed sons. The vast majority of moaning seems to come from parents who struggle with their strong-willed *daughters.*

Is there something greater at work here in our understanding? Perhaps there is some misconception about inner strength and to whom it should largely be ascribed to (boys)? Is it that when a strong will falls into the mindset of a girl we aren't comfortable with it?

Little boys are supposed to be leaders. Little girls are supposed to be followers. Little boys who display a strong will are commanding. Little girls who display a strong will are bossy. Little boys are turning into men, little girls are becoming difficult.

If we as parents continue to discount a little girl and her God-given ability to lead, we may well be depriving this generation of its own Miriam (Moses's sister, Genesis), Huldah (2 Chronicles 34:22), Deborah (Judges 4-5), Rahab (Joshua 2-6), Abigail (1 Samuel 25), Tamar (Genesis 38), Lydia (Acts 16), and multitudes of other leading women mentioned in Acts 17. That would be a tragedy.

Truthfully, everyone must learn to obey someone...even if ultimately, it is only God. But God is not simply interested in our obedience. He is interested in our relationship with him. And while obedience to Him and His Word is a component of that relationship, it is not the sum total of it. Just like the obedience of our children is one component of our relationship with our child, but our love is never based solely on that aspect alone. So my final word on strong-willed children is that we must pay attention to how we use that description. A strong will is really something to be admired, not bemoaned or detested. If we see that we consistently grumble about our strong-willed daughter, and we find these same attributes in one of our sons and we admire the traits in a young boy, we have to ask ourselves what is so bad about a little girl who is born to lead? Perhaps it is not the fact that we have a strong-willed child that bothers us. Maybe it's the strong-willed female that really gets under our skin. In that case, the problem is not with the child, it is with the parent who does not know about the multitudes of female leaders in Scripture and forsee the same ability as a blessing in their little darling.

14.

Terrible or Terrific Twos?

Fathers, don't exasperate your children by coming down hard on them. Take them by the hand and lead them in the way of the Master.

Ephesians 6:4 MSG

I know two-year-olds can be challenging. I've parented fourteen of them so far! They can try us as parents, test our patience, and at times, make us question our sanity. Two-year-olds can be a real handful.

But if we only see the hardships of any age as we are parenting, we will never enjoy the journey. If we focus solely on how difficult raising a toddler can be, we will miss out on all the fun and total joy that comes with a two-year-old.

First of all, they are adorable. Cuteness beyond

words.

They are smart. All those times we said we wish our child could just tell us why they were crying, and finally at two years of age they can really begin to talk!

They are developing so quickly and we have a front row seat to watching the world unfold in their eyes! And last, they are still baby enough to cuddle and snuggle. Babyhood is leaving and childhood is approaching, but this middle ground called "toddler" is a short-lived, fast-paced, over-in-a-blink stage that we will look back on with fondness.

I know because I have survived enough two-year-olds to testify. There will come a time when you look at those two-year-old photos and your lip will quiver. Your heart will break. Your only fault was to blink and now they're grown. How dare we even close our eyes to complain at such a gifted and sweet time? When you look at your two-year-old and feel overwhelmed at the struggles they can put you through, remember that they are only that tiny for so long and this challenging time is meant to grow your patience and strength as a parent for when you will *really* need it...like in those teenage years.

No Child Left Behind

I had gone to run a few errands and left my big girls in charge. Knowing that the younger ones needed to burn off some steam, they took the little ones onto the golf course in the backyard. After a solid thirty minutes of exercise, it was now time to come in and eat supper. Everyone ran willingly inside to the dinner table.

Everyone, except little two-year-old Stone. He screamed and hollered, kicked and yelled, dropping to his knees and then plopping himself down at the top of the championship tee less than fifteen feet from my back patio.

He did not want to go inside.

The big girls decided that was fine with them. "OK, Stoney. We are going to go inside now..."

They thought walking away, pretending they were leaving him, would cause him to come running.

Oh how wrong they were.

When I got home later they relayed the evening to me. I stopped them as they told me this story and asked, "Have you ever seen Mommy do this?"

"No..." they replied. A concerned look was coming over their faces.

205

"And what did you eventually do?" I asked.

They explained that even though they were never more than a few feet from him, he never made any kind of move toward them. In fact, the more they feigned leaving him, the more irate he became. Until finally Glory (hands-down Stone's favorite sister) came and rescued him and effectively ended the standoff.

I congratulated Glory. She was right on.

We are human and we are flawed. And, yes, my wee ones throw temper tantrums and lose it from time to time. The only difference is that after parenting fourteen two-year-olds, I have a slightly more experienced outlook on these issues than most moms and can tell you unequivocally that it is not *if* your child will lose it in public, but *when*... and it's what you do about it that counts.

I see the "Fine Jr., if you're not going to come with Mommy right now then I'll leave you here" routine far too often, and I completely disagree with that mentality.

If you are one of those parents who employ this tactic, I am neither against you nor do I think that you are some ogre. I just want you to hear me out. Maybe I'll change your mind and maybe I won't. Either way, I'm willing to bet none of us ever have much luck with this mode of motivation, so perhaps thinking it through could prove helpful.

You see, I was a little stubborn like Stone. I once had a babysitter and her husband wait it out with me for five hours at a dining room table while I refused to eat lima beans. If I was right in my mind, nothing would change it. If I didn't want to go, didn't want to eat, didn't want to do something...pulling that "I'm going to leave you here" malarkey would have only enraged me and made me dig my heels in deeper. I could single-handedly decide to make everyone miserable as a kid. Hard-headedness was a gift I was handed in spades. And yes, now I see it as a gift. I'm hoping eventually we all learn to see it that way.

When a kid like that, especially a toddler like Stone, decides to dig in his heels, placing the ball in his or her court by "leaving them behind" is simply misleading. A parent thinking this tactic will make the child run and beg, "Mama don't leave me!" is being emotionally manipulative and tantamount to trickery.

First of all, we know a parent is not really going to leave their child. If they did that would be mean, neglectful, and dangerous.

Secondly, the parent employing this tactic is trying to get the child to obey by scaring them. Fear is never a good leadership method.

Next, obedience and respect is something that is taught and trained over time, but it's not likely any two-year-old fully grasps it! In a child's mind, the imagery or fear that if the child doesn't willingly obey his parent, he will be left behind, is just a horrific message to send. Whether my child obeys or not, I will willingly, lovingly, always protect them and stand by them! That's the overriding message we need to send as parents.

And last, most of the time that I have seen a child losing it to this point of refusing to leave, it can be traced back to exhaustion, misunderstanding, or just plain someone needs to take authority and move the child to the dinner table. Which, in my absence, is exactly what Glory did.

Once in his high chair with his sippy cup and mac and cheese, little Stone was as happy as could be.

How to Stop the Temper Tantrums

Have you ever been held captive by a toddler tyrant? Gotten them strapped into a stroller so you can run errands and they decide to lose it in the one store of the mall that is the absolute farthest away from the car? Ever been in a restaurant and the two-year-old goes nuclear in their high chair? Has junior had a seismic temper tantrum while going seventy miles an hour down the interstate?

Most times this becomes a habit when our child has gotten wind that we, as parents, can be held captive. They somehow sense that in public, our word is void. They have discerned in countless ways that in a crowd, we can be backed into a corner and our consequences for punishment are weak if existent at all.

So now we have to teach them that they are mistaken, and we won't be scared to walk out of any situation!

Try this tactic. Put on your party face. Get ready to rumble.

Get dressed, get them ready, and talk about how today we have to go to the mall to get Mommy new shoes. But here's the thing—this is a training mission, soldier! We know junior is going to lose it. We have no intention of buying any shoes. We will walk the entire mall knowing that, at any moment, junior will erupt. And when our child does not fail to let us down, then we will determinedly (shamelessly, boldly, smiling knowing in the end this will be worth it) walk the whole length of the mall with a screaming kid out to the car to administer "justice."

If restaurants are the place where little Napoleon decides to defy us consistently in public, then today we are going to meet a friend for pancakes at IHOP. At 3 p.m., IHOP is virtually deserted, so our collateral damage (hear: personal humiliation) is minimized. Put them in their highchair knowing soon our little dictator will rear his ugly tyrannical head, and then we leave that waitress a fat ten dollar tip for the cup of coffee. Walk out with junior to take care of business. He won't believe the swiftness of our action.

Put the child in her car seat. Drive the neighborhood knowing her earthquake is impending. When it does...pull right over. She'll never see that coming. Guaranteed.

All it takes is a few secret missions and the ironhanded rule is overthrown. The element of surprise and swift justice gain back respect and put a little bit of "uh-oh...that woman isn't capable of being held captive anymore!" into their minds.

I have had to do this with children as young as eighteen months who would decide to pitch epic fits in their car seats the minute I pulled out of the driveway, and with children as old as six. Become known by them as a parent of your word and gain their respect.

PLEASE remember context.

If your kid throws fits every time you are out around 2 p.m., likely they are TIRED and you need to get them home for a NAP. If it has been a crazy week and you have been on the go too much, at too many late baseball games for big brother, or the wee one is sick...please do not even think about disciplining that child. This little trick I have had to pull on all of my children is something I do when I see it becoming a character trait rather than a result of some factor which caused upset, exhaustion, or illness.

The Embarrassing Kid and the Foolish Parent

I've had my moments as a mom. The meltdowns in public places. The temper tantrums in the middle of a store. The smart-mouthed answer coming out when you least expect it. *And then, of course, there are times my kids behave that way, too.*

But seriously, we have all been embarrassed by our kids. The more I mature as a parent, I realize that "being embarrassed" is the wrong attitude. Now maybe some of y'all younger, less experienced but way smarter parents, figured this out a lot quicker than I did. It took me a good ten years. The truth is, our children's behavior is never embarrassing. As kids, they are going to flub it up, try things they shouldn't, surprise us with their unbelievable ability to try and hurt themselves, and in general wow us continually into saying, "*I never figured they'd do that!*"

We give them boundaries, and they have to test them. Over and over again. We give them rules, and they have to break them. Royally. This is their job: to test our resolve and ask us to prove ourselves worthy of their respect. They humble us, and at times humiliate us. I have had more than my fair share of humble pie. *And it don't taste good.*

Truthfully, moms and dads, our kid's behavior is never embarrassing. What is embarrassing is if we do nothing about it. Let it slide. Let it go unchecked. As parents, we have to take responsibility when we are at fault and respond, and teach our children to do the same.

I often see a lack of response labeled as "grace." Parents ignore the behavior. We may like to call it a "phase." We hope the kid gets through it. Many times parents like to blame someone for it…the coach, the teacher, the youth group leader. Moms and dads—it's our job. These are our kids. Our responsibility. There is a huge difference between passing the blame (or even blaming ourselves) and taking responsibility.

Then there are the parents (and I have been in this category myself...many times) who stand stupefied. Our "I *never* figured junior would do *that*" paralyzes us into inactivity. We take no action because we are afraid of making the wrong decision.

Listen, I have learned something valuable over the last twenty years. Our kids don't expect us to always get it perfect, but they need our response. They need us to hold the line. They need us to do something, even if it isn't the perfect response or reaction when they disobey or call us on the carpet with their behavior.

I've had kids call names. Throw punches. Start fights. Say bad words. Throw fits. Meltdown. Smart mouth. Outright do the exact opposite of what I told them to do. In public. In church, for heaven's sake! One thing I can tell you from this vantage point of experience—*they all try*. We just have to prove to them that they won't get away with it. We love them into oblivion, telling them over and over again that no matter what, momma's love and daddy's love is never at stake.

Our kids never make a fool of us. We only make a fool of ourselves if we do nothing about their misbehavior.

15.

Love the Person You Married

Older women are to teach the young women to love their husbands and children.

Titus 2:4 NLV

It had been a busy few weeks. Road trips, David's work was over the top, and there had been a lot of coming and going in general around the household. The basic routine had been maintained, but there was a vague disconnected feeling growing among the clan.

Then, for several nights in a row, little Verity began waking up. She would cry in her crib and whimper until we came and patted her little bum. At first I thought maybe she was teething, but Tylenol didn't seem to help. Then I considered that maybe she had an ear infection, but the pediatrician said she was fine. Stumped at why all of a sudden at sixteen months of age she was now waking up every night after having been a good sleeper since she was about three or four months old, David and I were really at a loss.

Then we realized that because of our busy routines, she really hadn't seen Mommy and Daddy together much in the past few weeks. David had been getting home past her bedtime, so most evenings, Verity missed seeing Mommy and Daddy spend any time together at all.

We decided to let her play on the floor for a few minutes after dinner while the table was being cleared so she could watch us catch up in the sunroom together for a bit. We were affectionate toward one another and talked about our day. She sat, pretty content, thumbing through her board books and wandering over every few minutes to get a kiss or show us a picture in one of her books. After about five minutes, we ended our little chat with a kiss and scooped up our sweet baby to give her a bath. For the next few evenings we repeated the same scenario and by the third night, she was sleeping soundly right on through.

Folks, marriage isn't always easy...but it's even tougher for our children to really know or quantify our relationship if they rarely see our exchanges and the affectionate displays. Our marriage, the foundation of their being, needs to be seen as secure. If a child senses some sort of disconnect between their mom and dad, anxieties, sleeplessness, and troublesome behavior are not far behind.

Our simple display of relationship for Verity made a huge difference in the quality of her restfulness and her overall disposition. It is with this simple story that I want to spend the final chapter devoted to marriage and the important role it plays in our parenting.

Date Night

David and I are commonly asked how we ever get time alone. I really love my children and, of course, I adore spending time with them, but if I'm not very careful, weeks can go by without any significant time spent focusing on my marriage.

When we had a smaller family, we would usually have a babysitter once a week to come watch the children in the evening. David and I would enjoy dinner out and maybe a movie.

Once Courson came into our lives, that changed. He was born so tiny and for months had a heart monitor and needed a lot of special care, so we began having date nights at home. Over the next few years, a "flood" of new additions came into our lives through the miracle of adoption, as well as a few babies I delivered, and we no longer felt comfortable leaving our brood of so many small children with anyone. I mean, really...who could I trust to babysit seven children, four years old and under, with five older children, none of them above fourteen?

That phase of our life took some serious care giving. We began to plan one night per week where we would get all the children to bed early (or at least on time!) and have dinner just the two of us. We would spend the evening talking or sometimes watching a movie. We generally either ordered delivery from our favorite Italian restaurant, or we broiled steaks and enjoyed them with a salad and baked potato.

The date night became a very special witness in the minds of our children as they would set the table for us after their dinner was cleared and kitchen cleaned. They would pull out the pretty placemats, cloth napkins, and the best silverware and china. Candles, flowers from the garden, sparkling soda, and music completed the scene. Many times, extra gestures would include candles in our bedroom, turned down bed sheets, and even pajamas laid out! The children really tried hard to make everything special and pretty for us.

Every once in a while, I missed the opportunity of going "out" with David. But I saw the great lengths our children went to in participating in our "romance" as their little hands and hearts went about making such a lovely evening for us. I was actually thankful they had the desire to see their parents' relationship flourish as a result of time taken on their behalves to serve us. Not having a regular babysitter (we had a few trusted friends in case of emergency or very special occasions) and enjoying a date night at home was a unique example for them of the time it takes to maintain a marriage relationship.

As you can imagine, our days are busy, and many evenings are filled with work not completed in the day. For these reasons and many others, it is vital to take one evening a week and stop to sit and enjoy conversation with our spouse. We need to revisit goals and encourage one another.

For many women, the sexual part of a marriage is difficult to maintain without feeling as though they have been listened to, or without that quality time with their husband. Our date night fills the gaps left throughout the week, as I know that come Monday evening, I will have a chance to really catch up and speak privately with my husband.

I encourage those of you who are in a season where going out for a date is just not possible due to financial constraints, time restraints, or even lack of a quality caregiver during your absence, to consider practicing a date night at home. Let your children participate by setting the table or prepping the meal. Talk about how special the time is that you will get to spend with your spouse. The example you are setting for them will affect their future marriages.

Like the time little nine-year-old Kemper wanted to show us the great lengths she had gone to in preparing our room for date night...she left a lit candle on our bed! I guess she wanted us to remember to "keep the fire burning!"

Spend time with each other and let your children see how special that time is. It will quell their hearts, give them confidence in your husband/wife relationship, and teach them the value of spending time with their future spouse. A date night at home can have positive generational effects lasting far beyond just an evening spent together!

The Best Way to Teach Abstinence: Your Own Sex Life

"Sex is dirty, filthy, terrible, and sinful...so save it for your husbands!" Says one pastor trying to make a joke out of how some churches come across in trying to relay the importance of sexual purity. The audience laughed. I cracked up, only until I realized how true this is.

Many times, the message of abstinence before marriage comes across as fear-mongering and unrealistic. Most young people have no idea what a healthy marital sexual relationship looks like. After hours and hours of inappropriate television and film content, music that lauds lustfulness, and dozens of "mini-marriages" in which a quick emotional attachment is developed and an even faster sexual relationship occurs, these youngsters are struggling.

The churches are doing the best they can. Sexual purity is taught in the hopes that a rage of emotional and hormonal desires can be hemmed in. While these sermons are necessary and even helpful, alone they are not enough to deter sexual interaction between teens or young adults. It takes far more than simply telling them to stay chaste until marriage.

As parents, we should model what we want our children to have in their marriage as a healthy, vibrant, fulfilling sex life. If they don't first see how rewarding a marriage can be including a loving physical relationship between their mother and father, what the world has to offer will win their desires every time. As parents, we SHOULD be leading the way.

So, how do we model a healthy sexual relationship? I mean, it's not something we "show" a kid to do, right?

Actually, it is.

It starts with plenty of physical touch and affection between parents. Holding hands, "muchas smoochas," a pinch or a pat on the tush... lots of hugs and embracing. Snuggling up together during a family movie night.

And then there are the "looks" that a husband and wife reserve just for one another.

The private jokes.

The sweet whispers as we pass one another.

And as the children age, a solid warning not to come downstairs after 9 p.m. or else THEY may find THEMSELVES embarrassed.

It is important to talk with our older children about the importance of "ministering" to their spouses...the fact that sex is something beautiful and something to look forward to.

The bottom line is, if we make what we have in our marriage attractive to them, the world's version of sex will have far less appeal.

He's Not Your Best Friend

Over and over again I see it everywhere on social media..."So happy I married my best friend! Happy Anniversary!"

And for many reasons, this is really bothering me.

Classifying the marriage relationship first and foremost as a friendship can imply that the passion is gone. We gotta keep the flame fanned or light that fire back up! If the bedroom isn't hot but the friendship's warm and fuzzy, then what we may have is an amiable roommate, not a husband. And when temptation rears it's ugly head (because there ain't none of us exempt) hubby needs to know his wife can and will fulfill his desires.

Of course it takes more than just being good bedfellows to have a successful marriage. But I want to signal a warning that without a solid sexual relationship it is difficult for men to maintain intimacy on a multitude of other levels. If that aspect of the marriage is suffering, the whole marriage is suffering.

Let me also state that if a wife has "fallen off the wagon" so to speak, the good news is that most husbands don't mind a good roll in the hay to get reacquainted! Don't let past worries or failures stop you from having a fun night tonight. Start over now. It's never too late and it can only help!

Growing up in Texas we had a common saying:

"If you fall off the horse, you just gotta get back up there and ride!"

So ride, Sally, RIDE.

Ladies, it's just an observation of mine. But if we're going to call our husband our best friend, we'd better make sure we're still his white-hot lover...in addition to being his nearest and dearest friend.

It Takes Two to Tango

But there are two sides to every coin, aren't there? As much as I would like to say "Just have a solid sexual relationship with your hubby," and BLAM! everything will be fine...marriage just doesn't work that way.

It takes two to tango.

I am going to share what makes many women feel comfortable enough to rock their man's world in the bedroom....even after more than twenty years. Ladies, if any of these following explanations seem applicable and could help you in your relationship with your husband, just hand him the book and tell him to read. The next part of this chapter may well put into words things you've been trying to communicate.

Security

It takes security. If I am scared about anything, it can hamper my libido or shut me down all together. Fear is in no way an excuse, but it is a valid reason to reconsider what/who is making me feel insecure. From my many conversations with women over the years, this seems to be a common thread.

Security about my body...
If I feel insecure about my body it can obviously be a damper. When Daly Kay was about six months old I remember David and I went on a walk one evening pushing her in the jogger.

"What's wrong?" he asked. He knew things had not quite been the same between us physically since baby DK came on the scene and it was seriously time to address the issues. First, he gets points for just asking. It took guts to ask a new mommy what the matter was and if he could help. He genuinely cared about WHY I had been less than...white hot...and wanted to help me through it! He didn't bang on his chest and tell me it was my obligation to fulfill his every desire or whim. He loved me. He talked me through it. He gently responded and we worked together.

Obviously, this many children later, his approach was...fruitful. And just to be honest with you, it took until baby number six for me to be completely comfortable in my own postpartum skin! So don't think these things come quick. Sometimes it can take years of encouragement. Yes, husbands, years. Not that you should go years between interludes...I would never suggest that! But it can take years to work through varying issues and the main point is that we never give up on one another and we never throw in the towel on the sexual side of our relationship. You've only committed to her for the rest of your life, so you have time to work through it, right? The other option, not working through it...is not a very good option.

Financial Insecurities
If I feel insecure about our financial situation— that too can really ruin a mood. If I feel that our

financial security is at risk, I become preoccupied. I need his reassurance, even after twenty-plus years, that everything is going to be OK. I need to be reassured he will do whatever it takes. And he always has, which is very freeing. In many, many ways.

These are some of the insecurities that have affected me over the years, your wife likely has her own fears or concerns. Those I have listed are ones that I have heard commonly over the years of encouraging women in their marriages. Wise is the man who takes time to learn what his wife's struggles or hindrances are and then seeks to console them. That is how you love a woman through her issues.

Insecurities are best handled with loving protection and encouragement. A husband can protect his wife's self image by keeping his eyes away from pornography. He can speak encouragingly to her about her physical shape and be thankful for the miracles of life she has brought forth. He can be patient and understanding while encouraging her postpartum, or otherwise, to work through their challenges in the bedroom.

Communication

A woman has got to be talked to. Communicated

with. Looked in the eyes. You may not need to have coffee together or warm up to the idea of sex, but most women I know have a tough time opening up physically if they haven't been given the opportunity to open up emotionally through conversation. Ladies want the pillow talk first, not after. Plus, we all know y'all are going to be snoring in less than five minutes after the party anyhow. Talk to us. When you open up to us in conversation, we open up in the bedroom.

For me, if I know my man will provide, protect, and communicate with me out of love, devotion and respect, I'm ready to ride.

I share these thoughts on love and marriage in Verity's chapter because after twenty-two years of marriage and fifteen children I've learned a lot along the way. I'm reminded of the verse in Titus 2:4 which says, "Older women are to teach the young women to love their husbands and children." (NLV) I suppose being in my forties qualifies me somewhat as "older" and what it also implies is that it takes someone teaching you how to love your husband and children. I've learned what real love looks like through watching other marriages further down the road than David and I, through learning God's word, and through plenty of mistakes. If I can encourage you in that way by sharing some of my experiences in this chapter and throughout the book, then I have followed the mandate that God asks of me in Titus 2. Loving can take some learning once the wedding bells stop ringing and the babies start crying! I'm here to tell you it's all worth it. Keep marching, keep praying, keep leaning in and seeking His wisdom at every turn, and reap the rewards and joy that come from being able to say, "I have no greater joy than to hear that my children walk in truth." (3 John 1:4 KJV)

CONCLUSION:
My Prayer for You

'For I know the plans I have for you,' declares the Lord, 'Plans to prosper you and not to harm you, plans to give you hope and a future.'
Jeremiah 29:11 NIV

I am passionately patriotic. I love my country. I bleed red, white, and blue. I cry every time I hear the *Star-Spangled Banner* and pray for our leaders and those in the military.

I began my parenting journey anxiously, wanting to get this job right. Over time, I met so many other families with the same desperate desire that I started to believe that God could use all of our families to do something amazing in our country.

And I've been praying for each of you ever since.

So in concluding this book, I want to let you in on some of those prayers. Please know that I believe with you. I believe *in* you. And I believe in a God who loves all of us infinitely and waits ready to answer our prayers and generously give us wisdom. I look forward to spending more time with you in future books, as we travel and speak, and through our website www.TheRebacks.com. But until then, here is my prayer:

Dear Heavenly Father,

I thank You so very much for the privilege to speak into these parents' lives. I thank You for all the things you have taught us through various challenges and trials in our own parenting. I know You want to do an amazing work in the families across this great nation and I pray that You would shower them with Your presence, Your love, grace, and mercy as they continue in their journey as moms and dads. Grant them incredible wisdom! Give them confidence and help! We need your guidance and Your Spirit so that, through our families, You can bring hope and help to a hurting world!

Lord, I pray for an anointing over these moms and dads as they continue to grow in an understanding of who You are and then teach it to their children. I pray for them to hear Your voice above all others, that they would know the loving words of their Shepherd. I pray for an increase of love and communication in their families. I pray over their marriages. I pray for the friendships their children will make and the educational decisions You will help these parents with. I ask You to protect these families and provide for them. I ask You, Lord, to repair and restore the cracked and broken places in their lives. I pray You would revive their faith when they are tired and weak, and strengthen them with Your loving grace when they feel overwhelmed.

I speak truth over them when the enemy comes in to confuse.

I speak faith over them when doubts come clouding.

I speak health over them in their minds and bodies.

I pray You would give them fight in their spirit when they are tempted to give up.

And I believe You, God, for great things in the lives of these precious families in the name above all others, Jesus Christ. Amen.

Meet the Rebacks

Mom and I always take the tim
to have our coffee together in
the morning. That's when I'm
able to talk to her about my life
long dreams and just our plan
for the day.

-Daly Kay, 2

My favorite thing about mom i
that she's a fighter.

-Ryli, 1

I love how Mom always support
my independent personality,
and always tells me to go for
what I want in life.

-Bliss, 1

My favorite thing about Mom is how much she believes in me.

-Kemper, 14

I love keeping Mom company when she puts on her makeup.

-Glory, 13

I love how she never gives up.

-Trinity, 11

*I love how Mama takes care o
us. She's the best mama ever.*

-Courson, 1

*I love Mommy because she
always shares her candy
with me.*

-Liberty, 9

*I just love seeing her smile. And
our special dates together. It's
not about getting things, it's my
special time with her.*

-Judson, 8

My favorite thing about Mommy is that she's happy all the time. And she's never been wrong.

-Shepherd, 8

I love how Mommy gives us kisses every single night.

-Ransom, 6

My favorite thing about Mommy is the way she loves me.

-Soji, 6

I love when Mommy does my makeup and my hair...Oh, and when she gives me her perfumes.

-Victory, 4

I love you, Mommy!

-Stone, 3

Mommy, I hold you!

-Verity, 17 months

Acknowledgements

To my husband David—Who else would walk this road with me? You have shown me the best of what love can be this side of heaven. Thank you for all your encouragement and belief in me along the way. I would never have known what the love of Jesus could feel like had you not shown me true unconditional love over the last twenty-two years. I love you more each and every day and thank God for the gift of you!

To my precious children—You have made me a stronger woman and taught me about the love and grace of Jesus as I have grown up with you these past twenty years. Each and every one of you is a precious gift from God and has brought so much joy into our lives! Thank you for your patience throughout this book-writing project and for your constant encouragement.

To my paternal grandfather, Carl Wallace Johnson—Thank you for your hard work that was a down payment on my education! Your faith in a little girl you barely knew gives me strength I draw from daily. And to my maternal grandmother, Frances St-Ours, your prayers are the strong shoulders I stand upon. Thank you for always remembering my family in your supplications.

To my parents—Daddy, I know you're looking down from Heaven and I hope you're proud of all you see. I think about you every day. Mommy, thank you for always showing me by example what hard work and a marriage that endures looks like. I love you both very much and I am thankful for all you sacrificed to give me an excellent education and a solid start in life.

To my father-in-law, Paul Reback—Thank you for raising an incredible man in David and for loving and encouraging our children. From football games to swim meets and track practice, you're always there. I love you for that. And I've kept that birthday card you wrote for me...your loving words are a treasure in my heart.

To my mother-in-law, Sheri Reback—You and I are more alike than I think we realized twenty-two years ago. We love fiercely, fight hard, and believe the best even in the worst of circumstances. You have always encouraged us and been there for our family through the toughest times, and I know you'd do absolutely anything for your children and grandchildren. Thank you for instilling that in my husband.

To the one and only Kristine Webb—Without you, where would we be? You have been my co-pilot and helper every step of the way. Friend, daughter, executive assistant, cheerleader, prayer warrior... such a sweet and very real help you have been! Thank you for believing with me!

To my sister-next-door Suzy Welch—Without your encouragement, this book would not have happened. You have pushed me to think farther, dream bigger, and work harder in so many ways that I can't even begin to thank you enough. So glad God made us neighbors and that we became sisters.

To my sweet Leila Macauley—Thank you for loving on and believing in me and sacrificing so much for this book to happen. I'm grateful to be across the street from you and for how you've always kept your door and heart open to my family.

To my faithful friends and prayer warriors: Amanda Yannotta, Cheryl Plourde, and Amy Zwayer...you all held my family up in prayer and strengthened me when I felt weak. Thank you for being such strong supporters and listening to and encouraging me every step of the way.

Biblical Citations